LUKE STREET

LUKE STREET

Housing Policy, Conflict and the Creation of
the Delinquent Area

OWEN GILL

First published 1977 by
THE MACMILLAN PRESS LTD
London and Basingstoke
Associated companies in Delhi Dublin Hong Kong Johannesburg
Lagos Melbourne New York Singapore and Tokyo

ISBN 0 333 22058 7 (hard cover)
0 333 22059 5 (paper cover)

Photoset, printed and bound in Great Britain by
R. J. ACFORD LTD
Industrial Estate, Chichester, Sussex

For my Parents

'Paradoxically, as the rationalisation of urban life continues, boundaries enclose some lives more tightly, isolating and making them more alien and obscure, inspiring illusions about them, making them more vulnerable. Urban ethnographers can explore spaces forgotten or given up for lost, replacing illusions with maps of social reality. By rediscovering the lives of people in those spaces, by replacing stereotypes about them with descriptions that convey their vitality, dignity and humanity, ethnographers may restore some lost relationships in urban milieux, and in a modest way reduce the isolation.'

Vic Walters, *Dreadful Enclosures: Detoxifying an Urban Myth*, 1972

CONTENTS

LIST OF TABLES

PREFACE

The research on which this book is based started as an attempt to understand the lifestyle of a group of boys who regularly came into contact with the police and courts. In the five years since the project began my perspective has changed. I have been drawn into issues of housing policy, policing and urban stereotyping in an attempt to understand the production of the behaviour that comes to be officially registered as delinquent. The book is therefore as much, if not more, about how the policy-makers react to deviant minorities as it is about how the members of those minorities react to the wider world.

Just as my perspective has changed so also has the anticipated readership of this book changed. I had originally intended to produce a monograph written for other academics. That is not now my purpose. I hope that the study will be relevant not only to sociologists but also to the people who play a part in the creation of the delinquent area – the town planners, the housing officials, the police, the social workers and the journalists.

The project was completed between 1971 and 1975, during which time I was employed in the department of sociology, Liverpool University. I am grateful for the help of a great many friends and colleagues – particularly Howard Parker, Mavis Penman, Phil Scratton, John Mays, Joey Wharton, Noel Boaden, Ken Roberts, David Lowson, Jim Essex, Clive Davies, Shaie Selzer and Geoff Pearson. I am also of course indebted to Bugsy and Tari, without whom the project would never have been finished, and to Dorothy Lewis, who changed scribblings into typescript. But naturally my biggest debt of gratitude is to the people of Luke Street, who must remain anonymous. All writers are apprehensive about their subjects' reaction to their work. Although the events described in this book will now appear past history to them I sincerely hope that none of them will think I have let them down or portrayed them dishonestly.

December 1976   OWEN GILL

1

THE CREATION OF THE
DELINQUENT AREA

The dominant perspective in post-war writing on delinquency
has been that such activity is a subcultural response to the
frustrations of working-class life. This perspective although
producing insights has diverted attention from other factors
in the organisation of urban life which are productive of
delinquent behaviour. Most importantly the relationship
between the power processes that locate particular families
in particular areas and the eventual production of delinquent
behaviour has been ignored.[1]

The spatial organisation of urban life was one of the prime
concerns of the early Chicago school.[2] Robert E. Park, the
doyen of that illustrious group wrote in 1929: 'the metropolis
is, it seems, a great sorting and sifting mechanism, which
in ways that are not yet wholly understood infallibly selects
out of the population as a whole the individuals best suited
to live in a particular region or milieu.'[3] The Chicago school
saw the processes of urban selection as intimately connected
with the production of delinquency. Yet since that time
'ecological' and 'subcultural' approaches to delinquency
have become more and more divorced in both American
and British writing.

The intention of this book is to re-examine the relationship
between the urban process and delinquent behaviour. It
looks at the phenomena of the delinquent area and how
it is created in modern British urban society. *By 'created' I
mean not only the way areas which support high levels of delinquency
come into existence. I also mean the way they are created in the
minds of those people whose residential location is far removed from
such places.*

To understand the creation of the delinquent area it is
necessary to combine three sociological approaches – the
ecological approach (why people live where they do), the
subcultural approach (the development of distinct life
patterns and their relationship to local social and environmental factors), and the social reaction approach (the effects
of classifying individuals and residential groups as different
or bad). Not only must these approaches be combined but
their effects must be seen as interacting and cumulative.

But my concern in this book is not with sociological
problems as such. I intend to look at specific processes which
occur in the creation of the delinquent area in Britain. Thus
in terms of the ecological perspective I concentrate on
policies surrounding the utilisation and allocation of
publicly-owned housing, in terms of the subcultural
perspective I look at the behavioural and attitudinal
accommodations of those people who are forced to live in
low-grade housing in the 'bad' area and in terms of the
social reaction perspective I look at the way in which various
controllers, administrators and 'helpers' deal with the areas
so produced and in so doing exacerbate their difficulties.

Instead of being concerned with abstracted sociological
issues I am therefore concerned with understanding a social
problem which affects people's lives. Looking at social
rather than sociological problems has become un-
fashionable in criminology in recent years. Mention the term
social problem and the academics' immediate rejoinder is
to ask who says it is a problem and who is it a problem
to? My answer to these questions is unequivocal – the creation
of the delinquent area is a social problem to the people
who are forced to live there.

COUNCIL HOUSING AND THE DELINQUENT AREA

One of the most obvious and significant ways in which our
hierarchical society operates is in our differential access to
residential space – in other words where we are allowed to
live. Broadly speaking, we are either owner–occupiers,
private tenants or tenants of publicly-owned housing. Yet
few enquiries into delinquency have taken recognition of this
fact.

A brief review of the limited number of ecological studies carried out in this country since the war alerts us to the importance of the difference between publicly- and privately -owned housing in terms of officially registered delinquency rates. Mannheim in his study of Cambridge[4] referred specific-ally to three new corporation-owned housing estates in relation to delinquency. He concluded that 'although exact figures are difficult to obtain there can be no doubt that these three estates have in recent years supplied more than their due share of juvenile delinquency'.[5] Ferguson in his Glasgow study[6] produced figures to show that 'boys from corporation-owned rehousing schemes used mainly to rehouse slum-dwellers are found to have a much higher incidence of crime than others'.[7] Morris in his Croydon study[8] found that two inter-war council estates had the highest number of official delinquents. Jones in his Leicester study[9] found that housing estates had developed as 'important centres of delinquent activity'. Spencer in his Bristol research of the early 1960s[10] found a marked clustering of adult crime and juvenile delinquency in three areas, two of which were housing estates on the periphery of the city. Wallis and Maliphant in a study of the London county council area[11] concluded that 'delinquent areas tend to be areas in which fewer people own their own accommodation and more people are tenants of the local authority'.[12] Finally in a recently published and important study of Sheffield[13] Bottoms and Baldwin have shown that rates of delinquency were consistently associated with types of housing tenure. Publicly-owned accommodation housed the highest number of officially registered delinquents.

The evidence produced by the above studies is neither full nor entirely consistent. But at the very least it alerts us to connections between the organisation of housing provision and the production of officially registered delinquency. And in seeking these connections we have to partially forego our reliance on American theoretical explanations for understanding the phenomena of delinquency.

HOUSING CLASSES IN BRITAIN

A 'sorting and sifting' mechanism operates in the British city, but that mechanism is controlled by different forces and different interests are at work. It is still however appropriate to use the ffchicago concept of the 'struggle for space' to understand the organisation of British urban life. Taylor has noted that 'whilst today there may be town planners, civic designers and social reformers who modify the naked-ness of such a struggle this has not simply ended land speculation, Rachmanism, discriminatory housing policies, or prevented the formation of ghettoes. The housing estate is as much the prduct of competition as the slum and may evidence a similar if not greater degree of social disorgani-sation.'A[14]

The most important exploration of this struggle for space in the British context remains the Sparkbrook study by Rex and Moore.[15] They argued that any market situation and not only the labour market can lead to the emergence of groups with a common market position. And on this basis they argued that 'there is a class struggle over the use of housing and this class struggle is the central process of the city as a social unit'.[16] Rex and Moore suggested that there are seven distinguishable housing classes in contemporary British society and that this class structure incorporates groups differentially placed with regard to a system of bereaucratic allocation: (i) the outright owners of large houses in desirable areas; (ii) mortgage payers who 'own' whole houses in desirable areas; (iii) council tenants in council built houses; (iv) council tenants in slum houses awaiting demolition; (v) tenants of private home-owners usually in the inner ring; (vi) home-owners who must take lodgers to meet loan repayments; (vii) lodgers in rooms.

In attempting to understand the process of competition in a mixed housing economy Rex and Moore attach crucial significance to the role of housing allocation policies in determining the social composition of different areas. Such allocation policies are seen not only as of importance in determining the characteristics of publicly-owned housing areas but also in indirectly determining the characteristics of others. In the substantive part of their study they argue that various aspects of housing allocation policy in Birmingham – particularly the five-year waiting rule and deliberate discrimination by the local authority against coloured families – operated to the detriment of immigrant groups and that the housing policies had the result of producing a council house–white–suburbia whilst immigrant groups were forced into privately rented multi-occupation areas such as Sparkbrook. Thus Rex and Moore argue that 'the crucial question then becomes that of the criteria used in selecting tenants for council houses . . . local councils are likely to reflect the interests of the long-established residents who form the majority of their electorate'.[17]

ALOCATION POLICIES IN PUBLIC HOUSING: 'TYPES' OF AREA AND 'TYPES' OF TENANT

Rex and Moore attached controlling significance to allocation policies in determining the relevant advantages and disadvantages of families living in and applying to live in publicly-owned housing. How do these allocation policies work? Obviously housing authorities are faced with housing stock which differs in size, age and type. Such differences are the result of perhaps thirty or forty years of local housing development and are likely to affect policy-making at the local level. But over and above this, localised professional ideologies develop in terms of how the available housing stock *ought* to be used – in other words who should live where. These bureaucratically produced and in most cases secret philosophies help structure the social pattern of our cities. What follows may not hold true for all housing authorities but there is some empirical evidence and a great deal of authorities but there is some empirical evidence and a great deal of anecdotal evidence to suggest that the pattern is far more common than has hitherto been recognised in studies of British urban life.[18]

My argument in this book is that 'hierarchies of desirability' develop both in relation to 'types' of housing area and 'types' of tenent. Through the processes of allocation this leads to a situation in which those whose economic resources are low and whose power is therefore minimal are allocated accommodation in areas that become increasingly disadvantaged.

The hierarchy of desirability in terms of types of residential location is the product of both the physical conditions of the housing in different areas and the social characteristics that these areas are perceived as having. In the public sector of housing, as in the private sector, different types of accommodation in different areas are either more or less in demand. Factors such as the age of the property, its size, its physical condition, its position in relation to places of work and recreation and the choice of schools the area offers, all play a part in producing a hierarchy of more or less 'desirable' accommodation. And council tenants in a particular town or city will be relatively well aware of the existence of this hierarchy.[19] Although some tenants in areas of housing shortage will be prepared to accept any accommodation, most will request specific types of housing in specific areas. The end result of this degree of choice in the public sector of housing is that some streets, neighbourhoods or estates are very easy for the local housing departments to rent out and others are often very difficult. Because not all applicants can be satisfied in terms of their initial choice of accommodation, housing departments are in the position of having to allocate directly particular accommodation to particular families. And local policies on these matters will thus have very significant effects on the social structure and the social character of the housing areas which are produced.

In terms of offering accommodation to families a number of factors will be taken into account. The applicant's choice of area is obviously the first of these. Attempts will be made to offer the family accommodation in one of the areas that they have specified. But housing departments also believe it to be their duty to take into account other factors. The family's ability to pay a particular level of rent is one of these. For those families whose total income is low, certain areas of accommodation will be regarded as being unsuitable. Housing departments not only see themselves as having a responsibility to their tenants, they regard themselves as having an equal or perhaps greater responsibility to the local ratepayers. This responsibility demands the efficient management of the publicly-owned housing, and efficient in this context means not letting housing to people who cannot pay for it. Thus families who are not able to pay the higher rents are not offered accommodation which is regarded locally as being of the 'better' type.[20]

Also, and most problematically, housing departments have the task of maintaining the physical standards of the accommodation that they are responsible for. The difficulty arises in the subjective matter of assessing what are regarded as a family's social characteristics. A direct result of a housing department's desire to keep the good property good is that an attempt is made to allocate the 'type' of family to the 'type' of house. Thus the 'good' property is offered to 'good' families and the 'bad' property to 'bad' families. Just as accommodation is categorised into a hierarchy of desirability so also are applicants categorised into a hierarchy of respectability.

The way in which this is done seldom comes to light. Because the allocation of council housing is often disputed, housing departments are typically unwilling to give details of how one particular family comes to be offered one particular house. This information may in fact be unavailable even to local councillors. The rules governing the decision actually to offer a family on the waiting list council housing are relatively well understood and are a matter of public debate. The applicant usually knows how many 'points' his family has gained and at what stage they can hope to be offered accommodation. But it is at the next stage, the allocation of a particular family to a particular house, that the housing department must make a partially subjective assessment of the characteristics of the family and offer them housing accordingly. Although not all housing departments operate the same practices and policies in this respect there is enough evidence to suggest that many do make a subjective interpretation of the 'type' of applicant. This subjective interpretation is likely to be a very basic one – sometimes perhaps no more than classifying him and his family into categories such as 'good', 'medium' or 'bad'. The classification is typically made by the housing visitor or his equivalent.[21] The applicant's home is visited and questions asked concerning the size of his family and where he would prefer to live. An assessment of the standard of his present accommodation is also made. But while this assessment is taking place the housing visitor is likely to be categorising the family itself as well as their needs.

The majority of applicants will, of course, be classified as satisfactory. Depending on the availability of accommodation they will be given a choice of areas. But with some housing departments those applicants who are classified as the less suitable 'type' will only be offered accommodation which the department has the least demand for. And the end product of this is that some areas increasingly come to have the accommodation which is offered to the 'worst type' of applicant. One example of this is the common practice of allocating homeless families – often families who have previous tenancy difficulties – to 'hard to let' property. The end result is that certain areas will come to have not only those families which the local authority regard as being of the 'worst type' but also those familes whose total income is low. Indeed there is a direct and crucial link between a family having a low income and that same family being regarded as unsuitable tenants. The standard of material provision, for instance, on furniture and children's clothes, may play a large part in determining the housing visitor's original classification of a family. The family that can't afford to maintain standards is regarded as the family that doesn't care about standards.

If the family has a low income – for instance if they are in receipt of supplementary benefits – and is classified by the housing department as being of an unsuitable 'type', there is a possibility that they will only be offered accommodation in those housing areas which the department finds hardest to let and which are regarded locally as being the 'worst' council accommodation available.

'UNDESIRABLE' AREAS AND THE PRODUCTION OF DELINQUENT BEHAVIOUR: FOUR POSSIBILITIES

Economic and bureaucratic pressures combine to produce the structure of the British city. 'Desirable' and 'undesirable' areas are created. What then is the connection between the area that no one wants to live in and the origin of delinquency? If we put the question in another way, some possible answers begin to emerge. Why is it that those people who have little power (and who thus end up living in the areas that others reject) are likely to be disproportionately involved in delinquency? At this stage I simply want to suggest four interconnected possibilities that might be useful in answering this question.

Possibility 1 The areas into which the 'least promising' tenants are put have the worst of everything. They have the worst educational and employment opportunities. The avenues of 'achievement' and 'advancement' are blocked. Adolescents in such areas are groomed for non-achievement. In this situation the wisdom of adhering rigidly and continually to a set of rules that do not seem to produce any benefits may begin to be questioned. Delinquent activity may be one result of this questioning.

Possibility 2 The adolescent environment (recreational and entertainment facilities, etc.) in such areas is of so poor a quality that it does not offer an alternative to a lifestyle which develops as one of its themes the possibility of being 'outside the law'.

Possibility 3 Because of the processes by which such areas come into existence life within them is of a disorganised and tense nature. The aim of individuals and families is movement out of such areas and movement up the hierarchy of desirability. Thus community norms which could potentially control adolescent delinquency are given little opportunity to develop.

Possibility 4 The 'least desirable' area tends to have a disproportionate number of large families. Such families are often desperate for accommodation and will accept such accommodation anywhere. Also large families may face considerable financial difficulties at the time of their application and thus to an outside observer might appear to have 'low standards'. They will be seen as suitable only for the 'least desirable' area. Because of this such areas may have a highly disproportionate number of young people growing up together. This exacerbates potential involvement in delinquency.

These are only possibilities at the present stage. They are open to investigation in the light of empirical evidence. We shall return to them both directly and indirectly later.

THE SUPERSTRUCTURE OF DELINQUENCY

There is however a fifth possibility which I want to deal with in more detail. So far I have suggested a relationship between lack of power, residential location, and delinquency. But the delinquent area is not only created by the structural forces of housing constraint and minimal opportunities. It is also created by what people think and do about these 'least desirable' areas. We have to look at the action of the definers as well as the defined.

I now wish to turn to the people whom I shall refer to as members of the superstructure of delinquency (the police, the courts and social work agencies) – that group of people whom the American sociologist Vic Walters nicely refers to as 'trouble workers'.[22] In a complex society work roles are highly specific. Thus some people spend their entire working lives identifying and regulating the deviant. We need to look at the definition of these people in terms of what constitutes delinquency and their resultant role in structuring the form that such 'delinquency' takes. I am therefore concerned throughout this book with what Edwin Lemert referred to more than twenty years ago as 'the mythologies, segregation and methods of control [which] spring up and crystallize in the interaction between the deviant and the rest of society'.[23] Specifically in relation to the creation of the delinquent area I am concerned to show that the 'controllers' or 'helpers' may operate in different ways towards different areas and thus play a part in producing high rates of delinquency or initiating behaviour which is then defined as delinquent.

It is the police who are located at the first and crucial stage of the process of defining an act as illegal and an individual as delinquent. The police, particularly in the case of adolescent offenders, are in a position in which they have to decide whether to identify the behaviour as deviant, and how severely to press for sanctions against the offender. The action then taken can be of crucial significance in restricting the offender's choice of alternative roles.

In relation to the delinquent area, I would argue that because the police are a limited resource they define certain areas as delinquent and concentrate their resources in these areas. There are at least two stages at which such police discretion can be of significance in determining high rates of official delinquency in such areas: (i) the decision as to what level of surveillance to give different areas; (ii) the decision as to what course of action to take with offenders from different areas.

I am not going to describe in detail the literature on this subject[24] most of which is American. But a tentative picture does emerge which suggests that the police operate in different ways towards different areas. Not only are different levels of police surveillance given to different areas but also the police are more aware of the possibility of delinquent behaviour in such areas. Cicourel describes this in the following way:

> when the police discover or are called to the scene of a supposed violation of the legal order, their sense of social structure and memory of past events in the neighbourhood provide initial interpretations as to what happened. The general policies or rules derived from police department directions and standing orders are connected to legal statutes by the background expectations, remembered experiences about the neighbourhood.[25]

The main point to emerge from the American research is not only that the police may operate in different ways towards different areas but that the effect of such police activity is cumulative. The police officer enters an area with a set of anticipations based on previous experiences of behaviour and 'attitudes' encountered there. Because of these anticipations he is likely to regard as deviant an action which in another area would pass as neutral. A self-fulfilling process is initiated.

The British evidence on differential police activity towards individuals or groups is limited to specific situations or specific offenders and thus can produce few conclusions in terms of an areal perspective. Several studies are however worth noting. Chapman in an interesting but largely anecdotal study published in 1968[26] argued that the incidence of conviction is in part controlled by the social processes which divide society into two groups – the non-criminal and the potentially criminal. He argued that the latter group corresponds largely to the poor and the disadvantaged who are vulnerable to criminalisation because of a lack of privacy,[27] a lack of education, an inability to bring pressure to bear on the police and their high level of visibility through colour or residential segregation. Basic to Chapman's argument was that 'in working-class districts the police observe crime on patrol or are called in to mediate in disputes, some of which may involve crime. In middle-class districts, the police patrol much less frequently and are called in generally only when there is an invasion from outside.'[28]

In research published in 1970[29] Lambert offers the most detailed examination of differential police activity in the British context. He develops the theme of the residential segregation of the police from the areas in which the majority of their work is located. He argues that although police work in the decaying areas is acknowledged to be more difficult and more 'interesting' it is accompanied by a rejection of such areas as places to live. Underlying this perspective is the argument that the most important aspect of police discretion is 'that which derives from police organisation itself in determining what level of policing to apply to what areas, how to deploy personnel and what significance to attach to certain specialised police duties in enforcing "non complainant" infringements whose prosecution depends entirely on police initiative'.[30]

Cain, in work published in 1973,[31] argues that the individual police officer needs to believe in a largely consensual populace whose values and standards they represent and enforce. The police are therefore seen as being the intermediaries who bring forward for punishment those people whom 'most people' deem to deserve it. And Cain argues that the city policeman tends to broadly subdivide the public with which he comes into contact into the 'rough' and 'respectable'.

Finally there is the important work by Armstrong and Wilson based on the Easterhouse estate in Glasgow.[32] Whilst not solely concerned with police activity they argued that young people were stigmatised on the basis of where they lived and as a result were excluded from certain conventional areas of interaction. They also suggested that the young people internalised the public dfinition of their area. The result of both the external stigmatisation and the internalisation of the delinquent identity of Easterhouse was to amplify the difficulties that the young people on the estate faced. In particular it led to a form of 'labelling on the street'. Armstrong and Wilson describe this in the following way: 'The youth who resides in a delinquent area has a good chance of being labelled delinquent. His moral character may become a question of open debate, and be challenged more frequently.'[33]

Again the evidence presented above is neither full nor entirely consistent. But at the very least it alerts us to the possibility that the high rate of delinquency in certain areas is related to differential police activity towards such areas. This aspect of the creation of the delinquent area has been largely ignored in British research. By arguing for a recognition of the role of members of the superstructure of delinquency in creating the delinquent area I am not arguing that without them there would be no delinquency or no delinquent areas. Such a reduction to the absurd is of little help in understanding the processes involved. But the definitions and actions of these 'trouble workers' may, if not actually initiate delinquent behaviour, then certainly exacerbate it. In doing so they play a key role in creating the delinquent area.

THE LUKE STREET STUDY – AN INTRODUCTORY NOTE

This book uses the case study method to explore processes in the creation of the delinquent area. I have combined description with theoretical discussion. To do this I have selected one small neighbourhood to which I have given the pseudonym Luke Street. Luke Street is part of the Merseyside conurbation. For reasons which will become obvious I cannot be more specific than this.

I intend to tell the story of the people I was working with. Such story telling is rarely undertaken in sociological analysis. In the search for laws of general applicability the individuality of different situations is not described. But it is only at the level of historical description of concrete situations that accurate insights can be gained into the disadvantages faced by particular groups. To tell this story I have used various kinds of data. I have utilised housing department records, police records, Press reports, interview data with both outsiders and residents and also a substantial amount of ethnographic detail based on life in Luke Street.

I start by looking at the socio-historical development of Luke Street from its construction in the inter-war period. I look at the way in which from the mid-1950s onwards Luke Street was used as a 'dumping ground' for those whom the local authorities defined as problem families. I then show that by the mid-1950s rates of officially registered delinquency in the area were becoming increasingly high and it was coming to be characterised locally as a highly delinquent area. I then narrow the focus of attention down to look at a group of boys in late adolescence who live in Luke Street. I analyse the conflicts and tensions of their lives in terms of the physical and social development of the area and its 'bad name'.

My intention therefore is to illustrate the difficulties produced for this neighbourhood by successive policy decisions and the action of successive groups of professional administrators and controllers. I suggest that it is only by such an approach that we can hope to get away from the sterile and tautological argument that the delinquent area is delinquent because there are more delinquents in it.

No two neighbourhoods are the same. Differences in historical development, economic influences, social composition and physical layout combine to produce the character of the individual neighbourhood. Complex cultural influences are also at work. Thus in describing Luke Street and its history I am describing a unique neighbourhood. And yet the processes of bureaucratic manipulation, stigmatisation and cultural accommodation which make Luke Street what it is today are, I suggest, common in the towns and cities of Britain. And it is these processes as well as the particular flavour of Luke Street life that I am concerned with in the following pages.

2

THE DECLINE OF
LUKE STREET

One is forced, therefore, to the conclusion that the causes
are almost entirely social in that over the years, these areas
have been used to rehouse the town's problem families,
social misfits etc., and that the process ... has progressively
snowballed to the present state where the very names of the
area are associated with all that is undesirable in modern
society.

Abstract from confidential housing committee report on
vacant corporation dwellings in North West section of the
West End of Crossley, July 1971

Crossley is part of Merseyside. It has its origin in the nine-
teenth-century development and expansion of its docks and
shipbuilding industries, and still depends to a large extent on
these two activities for its livelihood. Broadly speaking, the
town can be divided into three sections – the East End, the
West End and the central business and shopping areas. In
addition to this the post-war years have seen the development
of new housing and industrial estates on the outskirts of
Crossley. And beyond these new estates there now lies a
sprawling middle-class residential area. The section of the
town usually referred to as the West End is an area
approximately one-and-one-eighth miles long (east to west)
by five-eighths of a mile wide (north to south). It is partly
industrial and partly residential. It contains a total of 2177
council dwellings built in the late 1920s and 1930s, which is
almost 60 per cent of all the pre-war council housing in the
town. Only a few council dwellings have been built in the area

since 1946. The West End also contains a fairly large amount of privately-owned terraced houses built before the war.

The north-west corner of this end of the town is composed of a large block of walk-up flats named Cambridge Square and a group of streets known as the 'Saint streets' – Luke Street, Matthew Street, Mark Street, Peter Street, Paul Street, John Street, Thomas Street, Francis Street and Andrew Street. Focusing down further there is a small section of this area which is relatively cut off and comprises Luke Street, Matthew Street and the adjacent houses on the Dock Road. This small section also has its own pub – Casey's – situated on the corner of Matthew Street and the Dock Road. Throughout this study this section of the West End is referred to as the Luke Street neighbourhood. Figure 2.1 shows the geographical layout of this corner of the West End and illustrates the way in which the Luke Street neighbourhood is geographically distinct from the other Saint streets and Cambridge Square. On three sides it is bordered by main roads and on the fourth side by a busy train line. The neighbourhood is, therefore, in the words of a local resident, something of a 'traffic island'. And beyond two of the roads there is a dock and industrial land. A full-scale map of Crossley clearly shows this small area as having the last houses before a large expanse of industrial land.

Luke Street contains 34 houses, Matthew Street contains 13 houses and the end section of the Dock Road contains 22 houses. The Luke Street neighbourhood can, therefore, accommodate 69 families. All of these houses are of the four-bedroomed type. This small neighbourhood, by itself, contains almost half of the 'very large' council houses put up in the whole of the town before 1946. According to the housing report quoted at the beginning of this chapter, the houses in the Luke Street neighbourhood, like others in the West End, are built to a fairly high level of density and in 1971 were defined as being deficient in modern amenities. Many of them had limited electrical services, small and badly planned kitchens, badly equipped bathrooms – frequently leading off kitchens and usually without washbasins – and no garaging or parking facilities. These official pronouncements about the condition of housing in

Figure 2.1

Cambridge Square and the Saint Streets

the area can be supplemented by some of the comments
made to me about housing conditions in a survey I carried
out along with local residents towards the end of my
research:

Empty house alive with rats. We have no tap and the
corporation will not do repairs. This was reported nine
months ago. The house is very draughty in winter and

damp. The floor boards are rotted. The wallpaper is coming off the walls with dampness from the empty houses next door.

Hole in bedroom ceiling, sink coming away from wall in bathroom, toilet cistern leaking.

Dampness, sinking floor boards . . .

The external appearance of the Luke Street neighbourhood is depressing. This is in part the result of the number of empty houses. In 1972 eight houses out of the sixty-nine were vacant and boarded up. In the evenings the appearance of the neighbourhood is made worse by the lack of street lighting. There are also other immediate indications that this is a neighbourhood with its fair share of troubles. There is grafitti on the walls and some of the houses have wire grills on the front windows. But the middle-class commuters driving along the Dock Road see little of all this. The only thing they would perhaps notice about this small corner of their town is a large sign on the side of the Dock Road which covers an automatic signalling device to tell them how long they will have to wait to cross the dock railway lines. This sign reads: 'Out of order due to vandalism.'

By way of introduction to the Luke Street neighbourhood there is one further point that needs to be made. Crossley is a town with a high level of unemployment. This was particularly the case at the time of the present research and attention is given to some of its effects in later chapters. In the summer of 1972, the midpoint of the present research, the national average for unemployed males was approximately 4 per cent, but the figure for Crossley was over 7 per cent. Thus nearly 4000 men over the age of eighteen were out of work in the town. Unemployment rates were particularly high for young people. For instance in 1970 the highest number of boys between the ages of fifteen and eighteen registered as unemployed at any one time in Crossley was 231, but by 1972 this figure had risen to 420. The town's principal careers officer was at that time confidently predicting that some boys would be leaving school who would not be able to find work in their teens.

The arguments presented in this chapter and in the complete study have their basis in the characteristics of the Luke Street neighbourhood and so it is necessary before talking about the neighbourhood in detail to indicate why this particular small area has been concentrated upon. There is a danger in all sociological investigations that the sociologist himself decides the parameters of his study and this in turn affects the kind of analysis he presents. The sociologist selects the unit of study and then proceeds to invest it with self-determining structural and organisational characteristics. This danger is perhaps greatest with those sociologists who set out to look at 'communities' and then select an arbitrary definition of where their particular 'community' begins and where it ends. There is the further danger that by selecting, defining and setting apart his community the sociologist makes it immediately appear more out of the ordinary and extreme than it in fact is. Simply through the process of sociological selection there is a danger of giving the impression of a distinct group of people removed from the normal realm of experience. Dennis illustrated this danger in its most obvious form when he wrote: 'People seem to find it extraordinarily difficult to realise that mere living together in the same locality can result in a conglomeration of very little sociological importance.'[1] With these dangers in mind the reasons for selecting the Luke Street neighbourhood can be given. In no sense was it a self-contained community; its life was intertwined with the life of the rest of the West End. But the following five reasons justify its selection for analysis: (i) it highlighted and made obvious some of the difficulties of the West End generally; (ii) it was geographically distinct; (iii) it had distinct characteristics in terms of a highly disproportionate number of large houses in it; (iv) it was regarded by outsiders as being one of the 'hard cores' of the West End; (v) it was particularly associated by outsiders with adolescent 'wildness'.

HOUSING DEPARTMENT POLICIES IN THE WEST END

In the late 1960s Luke Street had come to be regarded as the 'worst street in Crossley'. By reference to official documents, local housing department records, Press reports and conversations with residents this chapter describes the decline of the neighbourhood. The figures presented in this chapter all refer to the sixty-nine households which made up 'the Luke Street neighbourhood'.

As practically none of the early post-war residents of the neighbourhood were still living there at the time of this study it was impossible to gain a detailed picture of it at that period. However the picture that emerges from people who knew that section of the West End well at the time was of a traditional working-class area. Certainly the West End had its 'fair share of villains' and it was a reasonably 'hard area', but if anything it was the 'better' type of council tenant who lived there. Prior to the building of the new estates in the 1950s and 1960s the area had some of the better publicly-owned housing in Crossley. The real 'hard cases' lived in the old slum districts nearer the centre of the town. In fact, conversations with local people indicated that considerable pride was taken in the appearance of the neighbourhood at that time. Some of the houses were referred to as being the traditional 'little palaces' at that time and I was told 'it used to be a great little street'. Mrs B. who had been living in Luke Street the longest at the time of the present study told me: 'People used to stop their cars at the top of Luke Street and get out and look at the flowers in the gardens. All the hedges in the street used to be cut dead equal. But look at it now.' And Mr L. whose family had moved into the Dock Road in 1938 said: 'There were just a few drunks up here then. That's all, just a few drunks.' Housing department records indicated that there was no difficulty in letting property in the Luke Street neighbourhood at that time. For instance, the following is from a letter written to the housing department in 1947:[2]

> With reference to your letter which I received this morning, if you could consider me for the tenancy of a house in Matthew Street, it would be suitable in every way both for my work and my children's school. Also my son has been demobbed and will arrive home next week from abroad . . .

This and other letters indicated that properties in the area were much in demand in the immediate post-war years.

The beginning of what was regarded locally as the decline of Luke Street can be pinpointed with a reasonable degree of accuracy. In general terms what happened was as follows. Up until about the early 1950s there was evidence from the housing department records that people applied specifically to be moved into the area. But with the beginning of the building of the new housing estates outside the town, and the clearance of older slum properties in the middle of the town, the West End in the 1950s gradually came to be the centre of Crossley's older council housing. It began to approach the bottom of the local hierarchy of desirability. Those families who could afford the higher rents and were regarded as being of the necessary 'standard' were offered accommodation on the new estates. But the families who were thought to be unable to pay the higher rents and who were judged to have kept less satisfactory standards in their previous accommodation were offered accommodation in the West End of town. Making the effects of this process more extreme – particularly in the case of Luke Street – was the fact that very few houses for large families were available on the new estates. The rest of this chapter plots these processes in more detail.

Table 2.1 shows the date of arrival of the families that were living in Luke Street at the end of 1972. This table, like the others in the chapter, includes details of those families who had been the previous occupants of the eight houses that were empty at the end of 1972. Details of two of the families were not recorded in the housing files and so the table refers to the remaining sixty-seven Luke Street families.

Details of the previous addresses of the sixty-seven families were also recorded in the housing records. Only one of the families, the last one to move into the area in 1970, had come from outside the town but this family had a number of previous addresses in the centre of town. The majority of the rest of the families had come from the slum clearance areas in the centre of Crossley.

Because the Luke Street neighbourhood offered some of

Table 2.1

Date of arrival of Luke Street families

Date of arrival	No. of families arriving
1938	1
1947	1
1952	2
1953	3
1955	4
1956	2
1957	1
1958	7
1959	7
1960	6
1961	2
1962	3
1963	3
1964	4
1965	4
1966	3
1967	6
1968	4
1969	3
1970	1

the only large council housing in Crossley the size of the families that were allocated accommodation there tended to be very large. Table 2.2 shows the size of the sixty-seven Luke Street families on arrival on which information was available. The figures include mother, father and all children.

Table 2.2

Size of Luke Street families

Size of family	4	5	6	7	8	9	10	11	12	13	14
No. of families	1	4	5	7	8	14	12	11	1	2	2

Thus the average size of the families that were sent to Luke Street was nine members. Altogether the sixty-seven families arrived in the Luke Street neighbourhood with a total number of 447 children under twenty years old. The actual ages of the children in the families that were moved into Luke Street is indicated in Table 2.3.

Table 2.3

Ages of young people moved to Luke Street

Age	1	2	3	4	5	6	7	8	9	10	11	12	13	14	15	16	17	18	19	20
No. of boys	15	11	12	12	16	14	15	14	15	13	13	5	9	10	12	8	10	9	7	8
No. of girls	15	11	17	13	14	14	16	10	10	13	17	11	18	9	7	8	5	5	5	1
Total	30	22	29	25	30	18	31	24	25	26	30	16	27	19	19	16	15	14	12	9

Total 447

The majority of the families were normal in terms of composition in that both mothers and fathers were living with the family. Only three of the sixty-seven families had a female as head of the household. In fact, the overall picture to emerge from these figures is that the typical Luke Street family was very large in size and normal in composition. Finally, concerning the nature of the families that were allocated accommodation in the Luke Street neighbourhood, details were available about the type of employment of fifty-seven of the male heads of household at the time of their arrival. Of these, 12 were in semi-skilled work, 36 were in unskilled work and 9 were unemployed.

These then are some basic facts about the families that were moved to the Luke Street neighbourhood predominantly during the 1950s and 1960s. During my examination of the housing department records I also came across evidence of the department's policies of allocation in relation to these streets. The confidential housing committee report referred to at the head of this chapter had been leaked to the press in October 1971. This document had stated that the Saint streets and Cambridge Square had been used to 'rehouse the town's problem families, social misfits, etc.' My examination of the housing department records specifically for the Luke Street neighbourhood made it more obvious how this policy has operated. Most of the folders on the families who eventually arrived in Luke Street contained a small printed check-list filled in by housing visitors. These check-lists had been completed at the time of the family's application for council housing or for a transfer of housing. As far as I am aware none of the families knew of their existence. The check-lists contained such categories as 'conditions of dwelling', 'applicant's room' and 'type of applicant'. Space was also allowed on these lists for general notes on the applicants and their families and a section was provided for the housing visitor's recommendations as to which area they should be offered accommodation in. Table 2.4 shows the information that was available on the check-lists concerning the conditions of the dwelling places of the applicants who were eventually moved to Luke Street and also their perceived characteristics. Because not all of the categories on the check-lists were filled in for each of the sixty-nine families the number of families actually categorised in each of these ways is indicated under each categorisation.[3]

Table 2.4

Housing department categorisation of families

Conditions of dwelling (No. of families categorised: 42)		Applicant's room (No. of families categorised: 44)		Type of applicant (No. of families categorised: 44)	
Very good	–	Very clean	–	Good	–
Good	2	Clean	4	Fair	23
Fair	5	Fair	21	Poor	6
Poor	18	Dirty	16	Require supervision	14
Very poor	17	Very dirty	2	Unsuitable	1
		Verminous	1		

Housing visitors had also made recommendations and comments on forty-eight of the sixty-nine families that were moved to Luke Street. Table 2.5 reproduces these recommendations as they appeared in the individual folders.

Table 2.5

Housing officials' descriptions of Luke Street families

1. Applicants are a likely problem family for housing department.

2. Very poor type of family. Luke Street or similar. Suitable dock area only.

3. Tenement.

4. Cambridge Square. Well known to various corporation departments as a problem family. Three visits were made, no access. Info. from neighbours. The family is very elusive. They are out all day and do not open the door to callers. I went around the back of the house and am sure this is a C or D⁴ case. The yard is full of rubbish and smells strongly. Two windows are out and cardboard has been stuck in place. The curtains look as though they have never been washed. Mr and Mrs — have no idea how to care for a house. But expect to be offered the best property. Refused to consider a house in Luke Street.

5. Rough type of family. Suitable West End only.

6. West End.

7. This large family will go anywhere.

8. Undesirable family for corporation. This family has every appearance of being a problem family. Rent arrears, dirty house and applicant off sick at time of visit. No effort being made in house. This family has no idea of rent payments.

9. West End.

10. West End.

11. District recommended – Problem (?).

12. N. S. N. P.*

13. House or flat, West End.

14. Tenement.

15. 'C'.

16. West End.

17. Dock Area.

18. Tenement.

19. Dock Area.

20. N. S. N. P.*

*Not suitable for new property.

Table 2.5 *continued*

21. Luke Street area.

22. Rough and ready type. Could only recommend West End and Luke Street area. Rent book unsatisfactory.

23. Cambridge Square and Luke Street. Very rough type of family. Home neglected and rent arrears.

24. Dock Road area would be suitable.

25. West End.

26. Unsuitable family for corporation to rehouse.

27. West End.

28. Tenement.

29. Rough type of family. Home and bedding in fair condition. Mr — has been unemployed for some time due to ill-health. She (Mrs —) is in hospital waiting birth of child. Would suggest dock area for this family.

30. N. S. N. P.* Applicants have every appearance of being a future housing problem for department. Mr — has no idea of keeping a decent house standard.

31. Poor type of family. Only suitable for town area.

32. Older type of property. Could only suggest Cambridge Square or Dock area for this family.

33. This family were a 'D' case from — Road. Since being rehoused they have made no attempt to improve their standard. The neglect of this property in the space of 5 months occupation is shocking. They have caused a great deal of trouble in the street for other tenants and owner occupiers in this area. Their children are unruly and allowed to run wild.

34. West End.

35. Tenement.

36. State of this house very poor indeed. Some of the beds literally stink with stale urine. The place is cluttered with old furniture.

37. Cambridge Square.

38. Old property.

39. Problem (she said 'Snotty little rent men: if my husband were here he would punch you on the nose' – rent collector).

40. Definite 'C' case in — Street.

*Not suitable for new property.

Table 2.5 *continued*

41. Tenement.

42. No new property.

43. Flat, Town or Dock area.

44. Tenement 'C'.

45. Not new property.

46. Tenement. Town area.

47. Dock area 'C'.

48. West End. Poor type of family but home clean and tidy.

Although the evidence presented in Tables 2.4 and 2.5 is neither complete nor entirely consistent it is clear that the Crossley housing department was operating certain selection policies in terms of the 'desirability' of their tenants and that the West End of the town, particularly the Luke Street area immediately adjoining the docks, was regarded as the most suitable area for the 'worst' applicants. The categorisations used such as 'C' or 'D' and 'N. S. N. P.' or 'only the Dock area' were diverse but the end product was that one area was being singled out as being the part of the town where the least promising tenants should be offered accommodation. From the data that is available I estimate that the policy began in the early to mid-fifties[5] – the period during which the first of the present residents of Luke Street arrived.

The criteria by which the individual families in Luke Street were judged were at best crude and at worst entirely subjective. The data presented above hardly suggest a sensitive attempt to distinguish the particular characteristics of individual families. It can be argued then that the housing department was artificially creating a group which it defined as being a problem and creating by its action a self-fulfilling prophecy. Although this argument is initially attractive, in that it fits in with a perspective of deviance as simply what other people judge it to be, it probably does little positive service to the people of Luke Street. The amplificatory effects of the policy need not be denied to argue that the Luke Street people *did* face particular difficulties. Irrespective of the way in which they were labelled – and it should be remembered that at the time the labelling was secret – the families were facing all the difficulties produced by large size and low income. In a sense then, the families that eventually arrived in Luke Street were a special category. But the key point is that their difficulties should have led to positive rather than negative discrimination. In effect the housing department had (i) selected individual families who were facing major difficulties, (ii) reversed the perspective, saying that they were a problem to everybody else rather than that they faced problems, (iii) grouped them all together, and (iv) left them to it. Such a policy can hardly be regarded as enlightened.

This policy of segregation combined with the type of housing in the Luke Street neighbourhood (the largest available publicly-owned accommodation in Crossley) meant that from the mid-1950s onwards the Luke Street neighbourhood came increasingly to contain families that faced problems. And it is fair to suggest that these problems were primarily of a material nature, resulting from the combined effects of large families with low-paid insecure work, and possible ill-health and unemployment. It was evident on comparing the housing files for the new arrivals in Luke Street in the 1930s and 1940s with those of the 1950s and 1960s that the previous group were thought to be able to make good regular tenants whereas the latter were not. In the records it was obvious that the 'poor' or 'rough' type of applicant of the 1950s and 1960s was primarily characterised by his inability to maintain the material standards thought necessary and to pay the rent regularly. The family which was a 'problem' to the housing department was a problem in this very specific way but was categorised in much more general ways. Thus the key fact about the Luke Street neighbourhood that was beginning to emerge from the mid-1950s onwards was that a group of families had been put together who faced considerable difficulties in maintaining the material standards thought necessary and were, therefore, classified as generally inferior.

The rapid changeover of tenants in the late 1950s and early 1960s (see Table 2.1), particularly in the years 1958

and 1959 when fourteen families were moved into the neighbourhood, set in train a number of processes. Not only did
the neighbourhood now contain a preponderance of families
who were facing difficulties in 'coping' but because these
difficulties were obvious and their 'standards' were regarded
as lower than those of the original tenants, many of the
original tenants wished to leave the neighbourhood.[6] Thus
the impetus for the process of change which had been
initiated by corporation policy was maintained. Many of
the original tenants took the same attitude to their new neighbours as did the housing department. Because of the 'bad
name' of the area fewer and fewer people were willing to
move in, leading to a situation in which only those families
desperate for accommodation were prepared to move to Luke
Street. This point can be illustrated by the following remarks,
typical of conversations that I had in the neighbourhood.
A middle-aged mother commented: 'I used to think they
were making up the name of Luke Street before I moved
here. I'd never heard of it before. My husband asked if
I'd heard of it and I said no. At the time I would have
taken anywhere just to have a place.' And a boy of eighteen
claimed: 'We didn't have any choice about where they moved
us. There were seven of us and the only reason they sent
us up here was that my brother's got a record.'

Because of the factors described above the neighbourhood
went into what was perceived by the original tenants as being
a rapid decline. The following letter written to the housing
department in 1962 accurately pinpoints the beginning of
this perceived decline and also indicates the problems of
bringing up children which were thought to be central to it:

> I would like to make an application for an exchange
> of house and district. When I first moved down to this area
> six years ago I was quite happy with the district and my
> neighbours but for the last two years things have gone from
> bad to worse. My children are coming in using obscene
> language which they never hear in my house. It is some-
> thing they have picked up from outside. The class of people
> who have come here in the past two years have made it
> impossible to bring my children up decently no matter

how I try. I am very dissatisfied at the moment. There is no
chance of any increase in my family at all but I still have
six girls to bring up respectable which I cannot do in this
district.

By the late 1960s dissatisfaction with the area had for some
residents become more extreme, and by mid-1972, 8 of the
69 properties were vacant and 27 of the remaining families
had officially applied for transfers to other areas. On the
transfer forms each of these twenty-seven families had been
asked to state why they wished to leave. As many as seventeen
of them specifically referred to the nature of the 'area' and
central to their perceptions of the decline of the area was
the problematic behaviour of young people in it:

> House alright, but don't like the area. Can't grow flowers
> and fed up putting windows in.

> I wish to move from my present address (Luke Street)
> because since I lost my husband I have had no peace.
> To live in Luke Street you need a man behind you.

> We are both unhappy about the effect this particular street
> is having on our children and neither of us seems capable
> of settling here.

> Son in trouble with police due to local environment and
> fear for younger ones the same. We want to go as far
> from Luke Street as possible to break contact with the
> area.

The desperation felt by some residents at this time can
be illustrated by abstracts from letters written to the housing
department. Again the over-riding perception of the problematic behaviour of young people is clearly evident:

> You must know what it's like to live around here.
> Hooligans playing football and throwing stones, breaking
> your windows, pulling your fences to pieces. When you
> speak to them you get a mouthful of foul language.

> I have had enough trouble and break-ins to last me. If
> only I was gifted enough to see into the future I would

never have taken this house. I would have held out for another offer. But I was only offered this house because no one else would have it, and I have been waiting for 15 years before I was offered my first key. I am willing to go anywhere as long as it is away from the West End.

The sooner I move from Luke Street the better, otherwise I shall be landing in — hospital [local mental hospital].

This area is the lowest of the low.

I would like to apply for the tenancy of a house in — which I understand is a vacant 4 bedroomed one.[7] In the past I have been in difficulties many times with my rent and I don't intend to make excuses as I expect you have heard them all before. The simple truth is although it is only February I dread the coming of the summer holidays. I am afraid I am not equipped for street fighting and believe me there is a lot of this in the street. I don't feel I have the strength to face another year. I rarely leave the house. My younger children are becoming ill-mannered and cheeky. Even the school teachers have noticed the difference when compared with my older children . . . I would be ever grateful to you if you could get me a house away from here. I wouldn't care if it was 100 years old and needed decorating from top to bottom.

I am still waiting to hear from you for alternative accommodation, as my nerves are an absolute wreck. I've come out in a nerve rash, with shouting at children. [They] continue throwing balls at our windows. If there's nothing you can do for me at the moment, could you please get someone to build a high wire fence in front of the door and windows as there is no point in mending windows to be broken again. Please let me know what can be done, as I would be gladly obliged.

These letters and the information relating to applications for transfers indicate, therefore, that at least a sizeable minority of Luke Street residents were highly dissatisfied with the area in which they were living. By the late 1960s the Luke Street neighbourhood had reached what can be regarded

as a state of uneasy stability. Many of the families wished
to leave the area but nobody wished to be rehoused there
because of its reputation and 'bad name'. Already some
houses had become vacant and the housing department were
experiencing very great difficulty in re-letting property in
the neighbourhood. Talking about this section of the West
End one of the department officials told me:

> It's impossible to let houses down there. Immediately
> people go down there they say 'what – I wouldn't live
> there rent free and a gold watch'. The rest of the areas
> in the town are alright to let. No trouble really. But
> it's a nightmare to try and let stuff in the West End. We
> beg them to go down there to look at the houses. We take
> them down ourselves to try to persuade them to move in.
> We even take them down ourselves in the evenings to try
> to get them to go there.

The extreme difficulty of re-letting property in the area was
referred to in the confidential housing report:

> Such is the public's reaction to these properties that they can
> only be let to the worst type of applicant; the very type
> of applicant in fact, who can only deteriorate further in
> such surroundings, and who will add to the rate of
> deterioration. Reasonable applicants will no longer even
> view these properties, the mention of the address is sufficient
> to evoke refusal.

The chairman of the housing committee was quoted in the
local press as saying: 'It's not uncommon for dwellings to
be offered to six or even up to nine applicants before we can
get someone to move in.' The situation had in fact become
so extreme that even tenants of condemned property in the
centre of Crossley refused to consider property in the Luke
Street neighbourhood. And this was at a time when there
were more than 3000 applicants on Crossley's housing list.

The situation was made worse because vacant properties
in the area tended to be 'vandalised' as occupants left them.
The same housing official quoted above told me:

We can't get them occupied, the vandals won't let us. We just can't get ahead with doing them up. We make arrangements for people to look at the houses while people are still living there. But as soon as they move out its vandalised and so people go down ready to move in, get there and say 'no chance'. I had a house one day – I estimated that it needed £120 spent on it. That was while the people were still living there. Next morning it was £1000 worth of work to repair it. Another house I had we bricked up all the windows and next morning they'd taken down the wall and got into the back kitchen. How can you fight against that?

This problem of vandalism and the difficulty of re-letting property attracted considerable interest in the local press. For instance, one report referring to the West End had the headline 'VANDALS MEAN NO TENANTS':

Vandalism to housing at the West End of Crossley is so bad that families due to be rehoused from other parts of the town refuse even to look at property there, let alone accept it. The area's reputation has deteriorated so much it is becoming progressively more difficult to let houses there. This depressing view of the West End and the problems of empty houses and vandalism was given by Crossley's Assistant Director of Housing, Mr — at Tuesday's meeting of the housing committee.

Because Luke Street property had by the late 1960s become so difficult for the housing department to re-let and because empty houses in the area were in danger of being 'vandalised', the housing department appeared to introduce a secondary policy at that time in relation to that section of the West End. This policy in effect meant that tenants were not allowed to be transferred to other houses unless they could find someone to take their place in their own house. Although one official told me he thought that if people had 'done their time down there and made a go of it' they ought to have been allowed to move out, this policy became a general one. During my examination of the housing department records it became evident that a standard reply was sent to anybody who applied for a transfer from the neighbourhood. The following is an example of such a reply made by the Director of Housing to a Luke Street resident who had applied for a transfer: 'I acknowledge receipt of your letter dated 1st September and inform you that as you are adequately housed I regret I am unable to assist you unless you are able to find someone willing to exchange with you.' But because no one wished to move to the area it was, of course, impossible to obtain a transfer. As Mrs D. said in a letter to the housing department in April 1971:

> I have asked you for a transfer or exchange of house as my family is growing smaller and this house is too big. But you say you cannot transfer us. But if I can get anyone willing to exchange you will see into it for me. I don't know any person soft enough to exchange for this area.

Supporting the housing department's policy not to rehouse Luke Street tenants were the various reports written on individual familes who had applied for transfer. These reports were made at the time of the application and were again the work of housing visitors. Some examples of remarks in these reports were:

> ... they are certainly not suitable for a transfer to a new four-bedroomed house away from their present district.

> Not suitable for good property.

> Not suitable anywhere else.

In effect the housing department's policy at the time of my study had produced a situation in which nobody was rehoused from Luke Street by the corporation unless they were sub-tenants or could obtain a recommendation from a doctor that it was necessary to be rehoused for health reasons – and such recommendations were rarely given. As Mrs C. said to me: 'All the 4 empty houses in Luke Street – the people have either gone to private landlords or else like Mrs B. they've saved for a house. She saved 35 years for a house.' And the policy was justified by the local housing department officials in terms of the problems of dispersal: 'If you try to disperse them you get into trouble about it. The neighbours complain if you put problem families next to them. The first thing that happens is that someone finds out they're from around there and they're shunned.'

This policy of the housing department, of course, increased the frustration and resentment in the area and led to some strange paradoxes. One consequence of the policy was that some of the larger Luke Street houses were grossly under utilised. For instance, Mrs P., whose family had grown up, lived in a four-bedroomed house with just her adult daughter.

Many families wanted to move to another area but none were allowed to do so. All realised that realistically they had to stay in the public sector of housing. Although they were not aware of the specific characteristics of the allocation procedures the people of Luke Street rightly believed that it had been housing department policy to 'put all the rotten eggs into one basket'. But the housing department felt that there was nothing they could do about the situation. Although realising in part some of the difficulties of the area they believed that it was 'the residents' own fault'. This belief was made far stronger because they believed the structural condition of the houses to be reasonably good. Their argument was that 'the area is a bad one, but the houses are quite good, therefore, it must be the people that make them bad'. This was in fact a very prevalent form of reasoning on the part of many outsiders whilst I was working in the neighbourhood. As one official told me, 'it's the tenants that run it down. It's not the corporation's fault.' This kind of belief is in fact one of the central elements in the spiral of physical decline that had come to operate in Luke Street. The corporation gave the tenants' lack of concern as the reason for inaction on the part of the corporation and the residents complained that the corporation's lack of concern discouraged them from taking any action themselves.

'THE DUMP FOR SOCIAL MISFITS'

The process of allocation described in this chapter was only guessed at by the local residents until late 1971. But at that time the confidential housing committee report was leaked to the *Crossley News* and they in turn gave it a great deal of publicity, focusing on the use of the phrase 'social misfits' in the original report:

WEST END PROBLEM FAMILIES HIGHLIGHTED: HE CALLS IT THE DUMP FOR SOCIAL MISFITS

The worst part of Crossley's infamous West End has for years been used as a dumping ground for the town's problem families and social misfits. Conditions there now are so bad that houses can be let to only the worst type of applicant – the type of tenant who can only deteriorate further in such surroundings and who will add to the rate of deterioration of the property. These staggering revelations are contained in a confidential report prepared by Crossley's Director of Housing and Works Mr —. The report makes it clear that although the area is subject to severe vandalism and comprises almost entirely high density pre-war property deficient in modern amenities, it is the council's long standing policy of concentrating problem tenants in the North West part of the West End that has brought the area to its present state. The policy has snowballed over the years, the report says, with the result that the very names of the areas are associated with all that is undesirable in modern society.

Subsequent issues of the paper continued to give prominence to the 'misfits business'. One issue in particular focused on the setting up of two petition centres, one in Cambridge Square and one in Luke Street and the possibility of a march on the housing department offices. This issue also carried a picture of a group of Luke Street families and children. Some of the children were carrying placards which read: 'WE'RE NOT MISFITS'.

The 'misfits business' dominated the *Crossley News* for two weeks. Although the paper took what it considered to be a progressive step in publishing the report and believed that 'the people should know', its effect was primarily to crystallise the image of the West End as the worst part of the town, and also to produce the image of Cambridge Square and Luke Street as being the hard core of the worst part of town. Not only was the area described in extreme terms as a 'problem' area with a 'bad environment' and as the centre of poverty: more crucially the report gave public acknowledgement to what had been long suspected – that the area had been used to 'dump' unsuitable tenants. The emotive use of the phrase 'social misfits' came to be central to the various press reports that appeared and behind this emotive use the original purpose of the report – the problem of unlet houses – became lost. Although the press reports quoted local residents as saying 'there's some good people down here' and referred to 'the hundreds of decent folk who live in the West End', the overall result of the reporting was an extreme picture of a problem area used for accommodating difficult tenants and problem families. The reports thus crystallised the neighbourhood's feelings of apartness and resentment.

OVERVIEW

In 1971 David Kirby wrote that 'none of the dwellings erected in the inter-war years has reached the limits of its expected life and yet, while the inter-war municipal development has matured in many areas into as pleasant a residential environment as is found in the private sector, in other localities it has the appearance of a twilight zone.'[8] The purpose of this chapter has been to examine the policies that had put Luke Street into the latter category. The local housing department's policies of allocation in relation to the neighbourhood and in recent years the realisation that such policies existed led to the spiral downwards of the Luke Street neighbourhood. By the time I started work in the area in 1971 it was recognised by both insiders and outsiders that the 'residue live in Luke Street'. In outline terms this process of social selection had developed in the following way:

(i) Children of original Luke Street families grown up by early 1950s and, therefore, changeover of tenants.

(ii) 1950s – new estates being built. 'Better' tenants given preference for new houses.

(iii) West End, and Luke Street and Cambridge Square in particular, come to be regarded as the less desirable areas of the town in terms of housing.

(iv) Also Luke Street neighbourhood had high proportion of the corporation's four and five-bedroomed property. Thus large families were moved there.

(v) Large families often face problems and are themselves categorised as 'problem families'.

(vi) Specific policy developed (mid-1950s) to accommodate 'problem families' and undesirable tenants in Luke Street area.

(vii) Because of this 'good' families move out of the area in the late 1950s and early 1960s. Rapid changeover of tenants at this time.

(viii) Highly disproportionate number of young people growing up together and resultant 'trouble' in the neighbourhood.

(ix) Image of area becomes so 'bad' families refuse to be rehoused there.

(x) Therefore, difficulty of re-letting property (and problems of vandalised empty houses) and so corporation not prepared to transfer families from Luke Street.

(xi) Late 1960s onwards. State of uneasy and frustrated stability.

My purpose in presenting the information in this chapter concerning the selection policies of the Crossley housing department has not been simply to attack these policies although it is my own belief that they are unjustifiable on both moral and practical grounds. However, the situation as regards allocation policy may not have been quite so clear-cut as the above analysis suggests. The issues are complex and the situation probably resulted more from ignorance of the likely results of such a policy and an unwillingness to make changes in accepted practice than a Machiavellian desire to increase the difficulties of the families concerned. It is also important to see such policies

in the context within which they operated: I am sure that
many of the residents of Crossley would have been in favour
of them had they known in any detail of their existence.
The need to segregate those individuals defined as problematic or who offend certain standards seems to be a characteristic of a society such as ours. Indeed perhaps even the
Luke Street residents would have agreed that it was necessary
to 'put all the rubbish together' as long as they themselves
weren't defined as being part of that 'rubbish'. At the same
time it is important to realise the practical problems that
the local housing department faced. They were dealing with
the legacy of a planning decision taken in the 1930s by
which the main proportion of the town's large housing had
been put in the one small area. As an official of the housing
department said when I asked him about the problems of
rehousing large families, 'there's simply nowhere else to
put them'. Also if the council had decided to allow the
Luke Street families to be transferred they would have faced
a public outcry about the amount of vacant and vandalised
corporation property. Finally the housing department were
in no position to reverse the trend of stigmatisation by
changing their policies because 'better' families refused to
go to the Saint streets. However, having said this I do believe
that the 1930s planning decision and the subsequent policies
were in large part responsible for the problems of the area.
For the housing department to say that the Luke Street
property could 'only be let to the worst type of applicants'
was a rationalisation for the results of their more direct
selection of undesirable tenants. Indeed the most apt way to
describe the residents of Luke Street at the time of my study
was as an assembly of strangers whose major characteristic
was that they were defined as 'problems' by the housing
department. Allied to this, as the information given in this
chapter illustrates, Luke Street was a neighbourhood with a
very unbalanced age composition. The large families of young
children which moved into the area in the 1950s and 1960s
meant that by the mid-1960s there was an adolescent
population explosion in Luke Street. This fact plays a central
part in the argument that follows.

The purpose of this chapter has been to present some

of the key facts about the Luke Street section of the West End and in doing so to establish a historical framework within which the particular problems of the young people of the neighbourhood can be discussed. My argument is that for an understanding of the dynamics of a particular area it is more fruitful to examine the way in which it has been *constructed* by outside forces and decisions rather than to conduct a static analysis of its internal *structure*. As Damer says: 'the unravelling of the process by which some neighbourhoods come to contain populations of the poor and the socially afflicted, as opposed to the comfortable middle class of necessity implies a dynamic historical approach.'[9] Thus besides analysing the general societal structures that affect young people it is also essential to analyse the difficulties of particular groups of young people in terms of the specific characteristics of the residential groups in which they have been brought up and which continue to shape their lives. In effect the forces that had constructed Luke Street had thrown together large young families and those families had grown up together in very difficult circumstances. The activities of these young people had been central to the perceived decline of the neighbourhood by the original tenants and the increasing external stigmatisation. Following chapters examine the interplay of these different processes.

3

THE OFFICIAL DELINQUENTS
OF LUKE STREET

'It seems funny they're all living so close together.'
Criminal Records Officer

I have produced a framework for analysing a particular sequence of neighbourhood decline and I have also described the historical development of the 'problem' area of Luke Street. But my main concern in this study is to illustrate the connections between the various policy decisions and perspectives affecting Luke Street and adolescent delinquency in the neighbourhood. It is now therefore necessary to turn to an analysis of the official delinquency rates of the area.

The information that follows is again based on the sixty-nine households in the Luke Street neighbourhood. This information was collected more than a year after the end of the continuous fieldwork period for two reasons. First I felt uneasy about actually approaching the police for information when I was involved with the people of Luke Street not only because it would have made my position appear highly ambiguous but also because it may well have coloured my perspective on life in the neighbourhood. Secondly it was necessary for the delinquent activity of the area when I was actually there to filter through into the official recording machinery. It is also important to note that the delinquency rates produced in this chapter are if anything an underestimate of the actual number of officially defined delinquent acts committed by the Luke Street residents. The criminal records in the local records office are arranged by name rather than address and the collection of the individual cases apparently involved a lengthy and complicated process of cross-reference. When the actual list of offences was sent to me[1] I was aware that several people in the area who I definitely knew to have convictions were not recorded. The number of offences recorded below may also be an underestimate because by the time the information was collected several of the boys in the area with a lengthy history of court appearances had married and left Luke Street.

RECORDED CONVICTIONS OF THE LUKE STREET FAMILIES

Of the sixty-nine families in Luke Street[2] as many as forty-one had at least one member with a criminal conviction. The pattern of this officially recorded delinquency can best be illustrated in diagrammatic form. Table 3.1 indicates the number of families with at least one member with a criminal record. Obviously there is a considerable variety in terms of delinquent and criminal record. Some families have only one member with a criminal record whereas others have far more. The following, for example, is the actual record of one family (no. thirty-seven):

Grandfather	1 offence (handling stolen goods – not recorded in Table 3.1)
Father	5 offences (4 larceny, 1 possessing offensive weapon)
Mother	1 offence (larceny)
Son	6 offences (2 larceny, 1 possessing offensive weapon, 1 assault police, 2 wilful damage)
Son	12 offences (8 larceny, 1 unauthorised taking and driving away, 2 wilful damage, 1 allowing himself to be carried in stolen vehicle)
Daughter	1 offence (larceny)
Daughter	2 offences (1 larceny, 1 criminal damage)

LUKE STREET

Table 3.1

Family members with criminal record

Family no.	Father criminal record	Mother criminal record	1 son criminal record	2nd son criminal record	3rd son criminal record	4th son criminal record	1 daughter criminal record	2nd daughter criminal record	3rd daughter criminal record	Total no. of family criminal record
1			✓	✓						2
2	✓	✓								2
3			✓				✓			2
4		✓					✓			2
5	✓		✓							2
6			✓							1
7	✓		✓							2
8		✓								1
9			✓							1
10			✓	✓	✓	✓				4
11			✓							1
12			✓							1
13			✓							1
14			✓							1
15			✓							1
16			✓	✓						2
17			✓	✓			✓			3
18	✓									1
19			✓							1
20	✓						✓			2
21							✓	✓	✓	3
22			✓	✓	✓		✓			4
23			✓	✓						2
24		✓	✓				✓			3
25	✓									1
26	✓		✓	✓			✓	✓		5
27			✓							1
28			✓							1
29			✓	✓	✓					3
30			✓							1
31			✓							1
32			✓				✓			2
33	✓									1
34							✓			1
35	✓		✓							2
36							✓			1
37	✓		✓	✓			✓	✓		5
38			✓							1
39			✓				✓			2
40		✓								1
41			✓	✓						2
Total	10	5	30	10	3	1	13	3	1	76

The following are the officially recorded offences of another extreme case, family no. twenty-six:

Father	1 offence (larceny)
Son	19 offences (14 larceny, 2 assault, 1 trespass, 2 wilful damage)
Son	6 offences (larceny)
Daughter	6 offences (3 larceny, 1 assault police, 1 handling stolen goods, 1 allowing herself to be carried in stolen vehicle)
Daughter	1 offence (larceny)

AGE AND SEX DISTRIBUTION OF OFFENDERS

The criminal records with which I was supplied included the date of the offence and the date of birth of the particular offender. In all, 429 offences were recorded against the seventy-eight[3] Luke Street residents who had been convicted. Table 3.2 indicates the breakdown of those offences in terms of the age of the offender at the time of the offence. Table 3.3 shows the sex distribution and related number of offences of the seventy-eight Luke Street residents with recorded convictions.

Table 3.2

Age of Luke Street offenders

Age range	No. of offences
8–18	261
18–30	150
30+	18
Total	429

Table 3.3

Sex distribution of Luke Street offenders

	No. of offenders	No. of offences
Male	56	378
Female	22	51
Total	78	429

DATE OF ARRIVAL COMPARED WITH DATE OF FIRST
OFFENCE

In line with a central argument of this book that residence
in Luke Street exacerbated involvement in delinquency it
seemed particularly appropriate to compare the date of
arrival of the adult offenders in Luke Street with the date
of their first offence. Tables 3.4 and 3.5 include all of the
Luke Street residents with a criminal record who were born
before 1945.

Table 3.4

*Date of arrival compared with date of first offence of Luke Street residents born
before 1945 (males)*

Case no.	Date of birth	Date of arrival	Date of first offence	No offences before arrival in Luke Street
1	1940	1947	1959	✓
2	1931	1965	1964	
3	1943	1966	1956	
4	1911	1960	1968	✓
5	1942	1957	1961	✓
6	1942	1959	1951	
7	1943	1959	1952	
8	1942	1959	1965	✓
9	1941	1969	1957	
10	1941	1958	1950	
11	1938	1960	1960	✓
12	1935	1960	1957	
13	1934	1952	1947	
14	1925	1965	1970	✓
15	1941	1958	1963	✓
16	1910	1959	1970	✓
17	1938	1959	1956	

The pattern indicated in Tables 3.4 and 3.5 is of interest.
Of the twenty-six Luke Street people with criminal convictions who were born before 1945 only ten had been convicted of an offence prior to their arrival,[4] and yet the majority
of these people were adults when they arrived in Luke Street.
The average age of their arrival in the neighbourhood can
be computed from Tables 3.4 and 3.5 to be 26 years of
age. This pattern can in fact be seen to be particularly strong
in the case of the female offenders. Of the eight convicted

Table 3.5

Date of arrival compared with date of first offence of Luke Street residents born before 1945 (females)

Case no.	Date of birth	Date of arrival	Date of first offence	No offences before arrival in Luke Street
1	1907	1947	1962	✓
2	1931	1962	1964	✓
3	1931	1967	1966	
4	1926	1960	1970	✓
5	1944	1958	1959	✓
6	1922	1963	1972	✓
7	1940	1959	1962	✓
8	1944	1959	1962	✓
9	1944	1958	1959	✓

females born before 1945 only one had offended before arrival in Luke Street. In fact several of the Luke Street residents had not been involved in crime or delinquency until well into their middle age. Three of the more extreme cases from Table 3.5 can be used to illustrate this point:

Case no. 4 (male)   Born 1911
Arrived Luke Street 1960
First offence 1968 (larceny of cash from prepayment meter)

Case no. 16 (male)   Born 1910
Arrived Luke Street 1959
First offence 1970 (handling stolen goods)

Case no. 1 (female)   Born 1907
Arrived Luke Street 1947
First offence 1962 (larceny from shop)
Second offence 1969 (theft from shop)

THE VARIETY OF OFFICIALLY RECORDED DELINQUENCY IN LUKE STREET

The variety of behaviour that comes to be regarded as criminal or delinquent has important implications at a theoretical level. It therefore seemed important to analyse the official records of offences of the Luke Street residents not only in terms of rates of delinquency but also in terms of types of delinquency. Analysing the list of individual offences in this way produced certain difficulties – the main one being that the circumstances of individual offences were not detailed on the list: for instance categories such as theft can involve a relatively wide range of types of delinquent behaviour and the seriousness of such behaviour. But it was possible to make broad distinctions between different types of delinquent activity. I have therefore categorised each of the offences of the Luke Street residents in the following way:

Theft (including offences such as 'larceny', 'going equipped', 'housebreaking and larceny', 'burglary', 'attempted burglary' and 'obtaining credit by fraud').

Property damage (including offences such as 'criminal damage', 'wilful damage' and 'malicious damage').

Personal violence (including offences such as 'assault occasioning actual bodily harm', 'possessing an offensive weapon', 'common assault' and 'threatening behaviour').

Assault on police officer (as above but specifically directed to police).

Trespass (including such offences as 'trespass on railway sidings', 'found on enclosed premises', etc.).

Disorderly behaviour (this category includes such offences as 'disorderly behaviour', 'drunk and disorderly', 'causing an affray').

Other (specific offences included in this section are 'allowing oneself to be driven in a vehicle knowing it to be stolen', 'driving without insurance').

I have divided the Luke Street residents with a criminal record into four categories for this analysis of types of offence: (i) males born before 1945; (ii) females born before 1945; (iii) males born after 1945; (iv) females born after 1945.

The types of offence of each individual with known offences are listed in Tables 3.6, 3.7, 3.8 and 3.9.

Table 3.6

Types of offence (males born before 1945)

Case no.	Theft	Property damage	Personal violence	Assault on police	Disorderly behaviour	Trespassing	Other	Total
1	2							2
2	11						2	13
3	6	1	1				1	10
4	2							2
5	9		1				1	11
6	4		2	2	3			11
7		1			1			2
8	1					1		2
9	8	2						10
10	1							1
11	4							4
12	1							1
13	4		1					5
14			2					2
15			2					5
16	14		1		1		3	16
17		1						1
Total	68	5	10	2	5	1	7	98

Table 3.7

Types of offence (females born before 1945)

Case no.	Theft	Property damage	Personal violence	Assault on police	Disorderly behaviour	Trespassing	Other	Total
1				3			1	4
2	1							1
3	1							1
4	1							1
5	1							1
6	1							1
7	2							1
8							1	1
9	2							2
Total	9			3			2	14

Table 3.8

Types of offence (males born after 1945)

Case no.	Theft	Property damage	Personal violence	Assault on police	Disorderly behaviour	Trespassing	Other	Total
1	13	1	2	3			1	20
2	6		1					7
3	9	4						13
4	7	1					2	10
5	1							1
6	1	1						2
7	5	4	5	1	1		1	17
8	2							2
9							1	1
10	3	1		1				5
11	4	1	1					6
12	10	1						11
13	6							6
14	16	2	2			1		21
15	7							7
16	5							5
17	2	1	1					4
18	8		1					9
19	11	2						13
20	4							4
21	1	1						2
22	4	1						5
23	2	2	1	1				6
24	9	2					1	12
25	3							3
26	3	1	1	2				7
27	2	1						3
28	2							2
29	1							1
30	12							13
31	1	1						2
32	2							2
33		1						1
34	2							2
35	3	3	4		1			11
36	3	2	4	1		1	2	13
37	2	2	3	3	3			13
38	3	2	2	1	1		2	11
Total	175	38	28	13	6	2	10	272

Tables 3.6–3.9 also indicate the range and variety of delinquent behaviour for different age and sex groups in Luke Street. As can be seen there is a majority of 'theft' type offences for all groups (e.g. 69 per cent for males born before 1945, 64 per cent for females born before 1945, 64 per cent for males born after 1945, 68 per cent for females born after 1945). But along with these 'theft' type offences there are for all groups a number of other offences of a non-material nature. The important point in this is that individual records of conviction tended to indicate a preponderance of certain types of delinquent activity. For instance, some boys have records based almost entirely on theft-type activity. For example, the record of conviction of case no. 30 (from Table 3.8) is:

Age	Conviction
10	larceny (2 cases)
11	larceny
15	theft
16	burglary/attempted burglary
16	burglary with intent
16	burglary
17	criminal damage
18	theft
18	burglary

Other boys had records based primarily on non-material delinquency. For instance, the record of case no. 37 (Table 3.8) is:

Age	Conviction
13	receiving money knowing it to be stolen
15	disorderly behaviour
15	common assault (2 cases)
16	unauthorised taking of conveyance
17	disorderly behaviour
17	disorderly behaviour
17	assault occasioning actual bodily harm
17	assault on police
17	wilful damage
17	assault on police
18	criminal damage

Other individual records showed a change in delinquent behaviour at a certain age. For instance, the recorded delinquency of case no. 6 (Table 3.6) above is an extreme example of this change.

Age	Conviction
9	larceny
9	storehousebreaking and larceny
13	larceny
19	assault on police
21	unlawful wounding
21	disorderly behaviour
22	disorderly behaviour
22	assault on police
23	causing an affray
30	assault occasioning actual bodily harm

Table 3.9

Types of offence (females born after 1945)

Case no.	Theft	Property damage	Personal violence	Assault on police	Disorderly behaviour	Trepassing	Other	Total
1	7							7
2	3							3
3	1							1
4	1							1
5	1							1
6	1							1
7				2				2
8	5			1			1	7
9	1							1
10		1	1					2
11	1							1
12	1							1
13	1	1						2
14	8		1				6	15
Total	31	2	2	3			7	45

This variety in officially recorded delinquent behaviour in Luke Street casts some doubt on those theories[5] which have suggested that particular types of area will support particular types of delinquent activity. It also alerts us to the fact that different individuals and different groups in particular areas may be involved in specific forms of delinquency and yet this specific form of delinquency will occur against a backcloth of a variety of delinquent patterns for other members of the neighbourhood.

SOME CONCLUSIONS ON THE NATURE OF OFFICIALLY REGISTERED DELINQUENCY IN LUKE STREET

I have not attempted to produce a detailed statistical analysis of delinquency rates in Luke Street. It would have been possible to use the data to produce correlations between levels of involvement in delinquency and position in family or age of parents, for instance. But the methodological validity of taking officially defined delinquency and correlating it with various personal and family character-istics has been increasingly challenged as a meaningless exercise. Instead this chapter has set out simply to record the rates and variety of officially defined delinquency in Luke Street. The statistics should be seen clearly for what they are – the number of delinquent acts which came to the notice of the authorities and in response to which action was taken. In the context of this study I have therefore presented the above information as a framework within which processes in the neighbourhood may be analysed. Obviously if our concern is to indicate the processes and pressures that lead to the officially registered delinquent act we need to have a clear idea of the number and variety of such acts in the particular context with which we are concerned.

On the basis of the data presented in this chapter certain conclusions can be drawn about the amount and variety of officially registered delinquency in Luke street: (i) a great many of the Luke Street families had members who had been involved in officially registered delinquency; (ii) arrival in the area appeared to be significantly related with involvement in behaviour which came to be officially recognised as criminal and delinquent; (iii) the largest age–sex group involved in officially registered delinquency were male adolescents; (iv) there was a relatively wide variety of delinquent behaviour in the area although the records of individuals often showed a preponderance of one particular category of delinquent behaviour.

4

EXTERNAL PERCEPTIONS OF THE 'DELINQUENT' AREA

'They've all got a bad impression of us down here. As soon as you say the West End, a bad impression springs to mind.'

Mr P.

Chapter 2 described the decline of Luke Street from the mid-1950s until the early 1970s. Central to the processes involved in that decline, but only dealt with indirectly in the earlier chapter, was the reputation that the Luke Street neighbourhood, along with the other Saint streets and the now empty Cambridge Square, gained during that time. By the early 1970s Luke Street for local people had been located and identified as 'the worst street in Crossley' and the 'dregs of Crossley'. Outsiders had produced a definition of the social nature of the area and the residents were powerless in putting their own effective definition onto the position in which they found themselves. Luke Street was seen to consist of an homogeneous group of people who lived 'down there' and whose problems and way of life were distinct. The residents of the neighbourhood and their behaviour were seen externally as either consistently abnormal or consistently problematic. The *whole* area and *all* the residents had come to be associated with certain kinds of behaviour. And against this belief the occasional protests that 'there's some good people down there' were relatively powerless.

There are a great many methodological problems associated with the analysis of urban reputations. A full examination has to cover the contents of the reputation, its origins, the way in which it has developed, its geographical distribution and its differential effects. Also certain specific questions have to be asked. Who says an area is 'bad'? Is it just outsiders, officials and the Press that see it in this way? To what extent do insiders perceive it in this way also? And in terms of the constituents of the reputation it is necessary to ask in what ways it is thought to be 'bad'. Is the 'badness' associated with particular groups or is it more generalised? And is the reputation associated with specific forms of behaviour? It is also necessary to ask what are the effects of the reputation. How does it affect the actions that outsiders take towards the area? How do insiders react to the reputation? Does it also affect their behaviour? And finally, of course, it is important to see the inter-relation of all those aspects of the 'bad' reputation of an area and the way in which such an identity can develop in a cumulative way.

In an examination of this kind one is faced not only with problems of data selection but also with the difficulty that the existence of such reputations is often implicit rather than explicit and indicated by actions rather than words. Policy documents, Press reports, interviewed officials, members of the wider community and local residents often do not indicate direct perspectives on different urban areas. And there is the further difficulty that the researcher has to attach relative importance to certain sources of information in analysing the nature of the image or reputation. How much attention, for instance, should, be paid to the Press as either reflecting or stimulating an image of urban areas? Research studies into the stereotyping of deviant behaviour have paid particular attention to this source of information, but this may have more to do with its accessibility than its impact.

But having indicated the dangers and difficulties of the sociological investigation of urban reputations certain points can be made about such reputations or images. Particular places, areas or neighbourhoods come to be associated with certain types of residents and as an extension of this with certain forms of behaviour. Cohen has illustrated in extreme terms the way in which places can come to be associated with certain events: 'Communication, especially the mass communicating of stereotypes, depends on the symbolic power of words and images. Neutral words such as place names can be made to symbolise complex ideas and emotions; for example Pearl Harbour, Hiroshima, Dallas and Aberfan.'[1] At the everyday level particular areas or neighbourhoods come to be associated with certain forms of behaviour. The common use of descriptive phrases such as 'a good area', 'a bad area', 'a rough area', indicates that not only do we make mental classifications of other people in terms of the social and economic groups to which we believe they belong but also that we take the process a stage further and associate different groups with different locations. Thus specific areas come to be associated with distinctive patterns of behaviour and distinctive value systems.

The most useful way to look at the social meanings or reputations that come to be linked with different neighbourhoods is through an examination of what have been called cognitive maps.[2] The individual has to make sense of the complex urban environment he sees around him. He therefore produces an internally consistent mental picture of this environment and locates himself and where he lives within it. In the urban context this mental picture or cognitive map is likely to be a mosaic of the different social meanings that are attributed to different areas. And if these cognitive maps are to be of use in day-to-day functioning they have to be relatively straightforward and relatively distinct. It is only possible to have a detailed knowledge of a small number of locations and yet to fit these locations into a wider whole it is necesary to have a mental picture of the different sections of that wider whole. The individual thus selects out of his environment to produce a distinctive framework of social meanings; once that framework is produced, new information is shaped and organised so that it can be easily accommodated.

Suttles, discussing the 'public view' of the Addams area in Chicago, has accurately captured the nature and purpose of these cognitive maps and stereotypes of urban areas:

any statistician could point out that most of the residents are not criminals, that pedestrians are usually left unmolested, that local children are seldom arrested and that the majority of the residents are neither Italian nor Negro. These observations, however, provide most Chicagoans with very little comfort; and they would probably only smile and add that these are only the 'official figures'. Most Chicagoans, of course, do not rely much on official statistics to regulate their entry into various neighborhoods. Statistics always turn every act into a gamble, public stereotypes convey a sense of certainty.[3]

In his more recent work[4] Suttles has taken the analysis further and described what he refers to as the 'defeated' neighbourhood. This he defines in the following way: 'It is a community so heavily stigmatised and outcast that its residents retreat from most forms of public participation out of shame, mutual fear and an absence of faith in each others' concern.'[5] Walters has taken the analysis of the defeated neighbourhood a stage further. He sees the development and continued existence of disfavourable reputations as central to the processes involved in the construction of what he calls 'dreadful enclosures'. He also links these reputations to specific administrative decisions:

> Certain milieux gather reputations for moral inferiority, squalor, violence and social pathology, and consequently they objectify the fantasy of the dreadful enclosure. In the United States around 1955 and after, changes in admissions policy brought new combinations of people into public housing projects, transforming these milieux and giving them a bad name that was spread and sped by the wings of fantasy. According to the stereotype, housing projects are loci in which sick and dangerous people drift together in a kind of behavioural sink, producing urban capsules of pathology so highly concentrated that the ordinary resources of the body social cannot control them.[6]

Following on from Suttles and Walters an analysis of the 'bad' reputations of different urban areas shows that these reputations have a number of important characteristics. First they tend to be the product of external definers rather than of the indigeneous population. Thus in most urban complexes there are neighbourhoods which are generally regarded by outsiders as being 'bad' but which the people who actually live in them perceive in a different and far more complex way. In an extreme form this discrepancy in perception can lead to the feeling inside such neighbourhoods that 'outsiders always look down on us' but 'there's some good people living here'. One of the most common examples of this tension is the resentment felt by people whose neighbourhood has been defined as 'delinquent'. Most people living in such neighbourhoods accurately perceive delinquent activity to be only a small fragment of the ongoing life of the neighbourhood and resent the external perception of continuous delinquent activity. This is not, of course, to argue that all residents of neighbourhoods defined as 'bad' will feel resentment about the way in which outsiders perceive them. Another reaction, and one which has a strong effect on the neighbourhood's internal stability, is that of believing the reputation is justified and wishing to leave. And finally some groups in the neighbourhood may use the 'bad' reputation to their own advantage and incorporate it into their particular style.

Another general characteristic of the 'bad' reputation is that neighbourhood identities, like individual identities, may be more or less crystallised but once a particular image of an urban area has developed it is unlikely to change. Information about the neighbourhood is selected by the outside world in such a way that only facts which fit in with the existing conceptualisation are recognised. Although insiders may think that a particular neighbourhood has quietened down in the last few years outsiders will continue to think of it as 'bad'. Thus a straightforward external stereotype is maintained and this stereotype cannot take into account the continuing diversity and change within the neighbourhood.

A final general point is that the more powerful the barriers are between the neighbourhood and the wider community the stronger the externally imposed identity or reputation of that neighbourhood is likely to be. These barriers can be either physical or social in nature. Within the urban context

features such as railway lines, tracts of industrial land or even
main roads can play a part in structuring people's notions of
where different neighbourhoods begin and where they end.
The stronger these physical barriers are the more likely it is
that the residential space so created will be regarded in
extreme terms. If the barriers are social in nature – for
instance if there are sharp differences in the economic position
of adjoining residential groups – then again the externally
imposed identities of each group are likely to be stronger.[7]
And these social barriers may be the product of less extreme
distinctions such as the length of residence of different groups
in the same area.

Underlying the way that outsiders view the 'bad' neighbourhood is a belief that certain types of people live together,
that like attracts like and that everyone finds his own social
level. If someone lives in a 'bad' area it is in a sense because
he himself is 'bad' or alternatively that he chooses the
company of other 'bad' people. And closely linked with
the external notion of 'like attracting like' is the perception
of the internal homogeneity of separate urban areas. The
individuals who live in a neighbourhood are perceived as
being similar 'types' of people who are likely to behave
in the same way. The stereotype takes no account of the
diversity and tension within individual neighbourhoods.
Central to the way in which the wider community views the
'bad' neighbourhood is the uneasiness that is felt about it.
This uneasiness is typically not the result of any altruistic
feelings about the quality of life for the residents of such
neighbourhoods. Rather it is the result of a general fear
about the dangers of social contamination and a belief in
the potential for conflict between residents of the 'bad' neighbourhood and members of the wider society.

Not all groups in the wider community view a particular
neighbourhood in exactly the same way. Certain groups such
as the police, probation officers and welfare workers have
specific roles in relation to residential neighbourhoods and
the people in them. These people tend to have more specific
images of the neighbourhoods under question but because
of the work they do and the necessity for believing in the
value of such work they are again likely to regard the areas

as abnormal. Because the members of the neighbourhood they come into contact with are a highly biased sample they are likely to adopt extreme perspectives. And although they may see the 'causes' of the problem this does not negate the basic perspective that the neighbourhood is 'abnormal'. Thus they may be concerned about the 'problems' of an area but this concern often produces simply a professional version of the stereotype of the abnormal area. Added to this there is, of course, a complex but significant relationship between popular and professional versions of the 'causes' of social problems.

The end product of these processes is that certain areas come to be associated with certain types of people and, as an extension of this, with certain types of behaviour. This process may be in evidence with residential groups of different sizes. So at one extreme large estates may have a 'bad' reputation and at the other extreme single streets may have such a reputation. At the local level these reputations may be even more specific, so that for instance one end of a street may be regarded as having different social characteristics to the other end.[8] And again at the local level certain specific locations may be regarded by outsiders as epitomising the type of residential neighbourhood in which they are found. Thus a street corner and the activity on it may be taken by outsiders to symbolise the characteristics of a neighbourhood.

IMAGES OF LUKE STREET

One aspect of the reputation of the West End of Crossley calls for special analysis because it was directly linked with the position in which adolescents in the area found themselves, the difficulties that they faced and the adjustments that they made. The West End and Luke Street in particular had over the years come to be regarded as a local centre of delinquency, vandalism and adolescent lawlessness. I am not arguing that this external perception of Luke Street as a 'delinquent' area was without validity. The statistics presented in the previous chapter indicate that many of the residents *had* been involved in activity that had been officially recognised as delinquent. But what I shall argue in later chapters is that this developing external stereotype of it as being an an area in which problematic behaviour could be expected became very extreme and affected the lives of adolescents in the area. In a very real sense it was part of their opportunity structure. The extreme stereotype was not only the *result* of 'official' delinquent activity in the neighbourhood but also played a part in the *production* of such behaviour.

It is impossible to gauge the exact role of the national and local Press in the production of stereotypes of different urban areas. Do they create or reflect stereotypes? How much notice is taken of the Press by the particular area in question? Like the examination of any communication process a great many untestable hypotheses are produced. But whatever the exact relationship between Press reporting and public stereotypes, an examination of the images of the West End portrayed by the local paper, the *Crossley News*, is important at two levels. First, it illustrates the general perceptions that the rest of the town held towards the West End; secondly, it indicates the particular aspects of life in the West End which the wider community found problematic. Also, of course, the local Press offered to the residents of the area the most definitive statement as to how the outside world looked at them. And this, it can be argued, was of particular importance in the case of young people in the area.

Research on the national and local Press has produced guidelines for empirical analysis which are relevant in the case of deviant behaviour. The most important of these is that newspapermen have consistent but rarely expressed ideas of what constitutes 'news'. To quote Hall, 'The process of news production has its own structure. News items which infringe social norms, break the pattern of expectations and contrast with our sense of the everyday, or are dramatic, or have numerous and intimate contacts with the life of the recipients have greater news salience for journalists than others.'[9]

A second guideline has been the notion of consensus news. It has been suggested that papers which aim at a general readership tend to stress the values which are likely to be common to all. Controversial issues are reported from the sidelines or not at all. And this idea is of particular importance, it can be argued, in the case of the local Press. Local papers have a monopoly of their readership and it is, therefore, sound economic sense for them to cater for all 'tastes'. Cox and Morgan in their study of the local Press and politics have accurately summed up one of the major outcomes of consensus news at the local level:

> They [the papers] were committed but to a rather innocuous concept, the 'good of the town'. Being considered self-evident, it was never really examined in any depth. At best it involved the attempt to foster community consciousness. At worst, it often identified the interest of a section of the townspeople as the interest of all. It was ... the local equivalent of the concept 'the national interest'.[10]

Deviant behaviour has a high news value and if that behaviour is directly linked with an obvious or implied threat against the 'good of the community' then the news value is increased. As an extension of this certain areas can be associated with deviant behaviour and thus the local press can be responsible for the over-emphasis of different characteristics of urban areas and the production of stereotypes which imply that these characteristics are common and consistent. The general implication of such reporting therefore, can, be that the behaviour and values of whole urban areas are against the 'good of the community'.

The most frequent picture that was presented by the *Crossley News* in respect to the West End of town was that it was the centre of adolescent delinquency. Vandalism in particular was seen to have reached crisis level in the area.[11] And it is important to note that vandalism was taken by the *Crossley News* to mean not only damage to property but any kind of adolescent behaviour of an apparently non-utilitarian nature that was regarded as problematic. For instance if a group of boys were involved in a street offence with the police they were also reported as 'vandals'. The *Crossley News* continually carried stories of its growing cost and the views of experts on how to combat it:

FOCUS ON THE VANDALS

Vandalism. The word gets more and more hackneyed every
time a window is smashed, a seat slashed, or a poster
daubed. But the problem gets bigger, the cost of repairs
higher and the police and officials more worried.[12]

In terms of the reporting of vandalism the West End was
often seen to be the 'worst part of town':

BORED VANDALS RUN RIOT IN TOWN

With the schools on holiday, Crossley is in the grip of
vandals. Since Easter a house has been set on fire twice,
acid released from a parked road tanker, the publican
of a vandalised West End pub[13] has given up and the
town council has got fed up with replacing windows.

The *Crossley News* also printed letters which upheld the anti-
social image of the West End. The following letter signed
by a 'working man' is a good example of the way in which
the stereotypes of people choosing to be unemployed,
lawless youth, and vandalism became intermingled when
reference was made to the West End:

IS WORKING WORTH WHILE?

As a working man and working almost seven days a week,
I wonder sometimes whether or not it is all worth it.
I see men who are out of work, in the same public house
every lunch and evening time, while their wives are at
the bingo, and their children, if not in school, are running
around the streets in the cold, or picking up bits of coal
that have fallen off passing trains, to take home for their
fire. You may think I'm exaggerating a little bit, but I'm
willing to bet a week's wages that it is the truth. Please
don't print my name as I live down the West End and it
is the wrong time of year to have my windows broken.

Some reports maintained the stereotyping of the West End

as being the centre of vandalism in more indirect ways. The following is an example of such reporting:

WEST END VANDALS: THEY'RE NOTHING LIKE OURS

A Crossley woman is asking to be rehoused in the West End of town, renowned for its vandalism and poor housing because of an even worse situation at her home in —. .

In terms of Press publicity one of the most important results of the official concern over the high rates of vandalism was that the Mayor of Crossley in 1972 took the 'fight against vandalism' as the main theme for his year in office.[14] Headlines such as 'VANDALISM PLEDGE BY THE NEW MAYOR' and 'BENCH NOT TOUGH ENOUGH ON VANDALS' appeared regularly in the *Crossley News* at that time. And as a result of the Mayor's enthusiasm to 'combat vandalism' he set up a 'Vandalism Committee' composed of three clergymen, two lady councillors, the secretary of the local council of social services, a probation officer, a warden of a boys club, a headmaster, the town clerk, the director of architecture, housing and works, the medical officer of health and the director of education. This was reported in the *Crossley News* in the following way:

THEY AIM TO FIGHT VANDALISM

A fifteen-strong team has been formed to fight one of Crossley's most seroius social problems, the seemingly uncontrollable amount of vandalism in the town. The working party . . . will concentrate much of their time on the town's vandalism black spot the West End.

The committee's decision to appoint a detached youth worker in the West End was reported in typical 'fight against vandalism' terms. The Press report that announced the appointment nicely illustrates the contradiction of helping the deviants and at the same time combating their behaviour:

A roving trouble-shooter may be appointed to help young people in Crossley's West End . . .

The various activities and suggestions of the Vandalism Committee continued to receive Press coverage throughout the year and its demise along with the departure of its chairman was reported in the following way:

THERE'S TROUBLE AGAIN IN THE WEST END

Two big peacekeeping forces in the vandal-torn West End of Crossley have pulled out. The town's vandalism committee formed a year ago to halt senseless violence and destruction has packed up. And stalwart community worker the Rev. — is to preach his last sermon on . . . Meanwhile vandalism in the West End continues.

In another article, the same clergyman was referred to as 'a quietly spoken churchman who used kindness to tame some of the roughest streets in Crossley's West End'. In the same week, the *Crossley News* carried the following editorial which although realising to an extent the consequences of the stereotype of the West End, still maintained it:

Crossley's West End is a problem area frequently in the news. Vandalism, violence and crime proliferate amid the terraces of rotten housing which dominate much of this part of the borough. The activities of the lawless ones fuel the view that this is the roughest, toughest corner of town. The young gangs respond in turn by living up to their ready made reputation; witness the streets strewn with glass and rubble, the pugnacious graffiti, the belligerent behaviour on Bonfire night, the disquieting crime rate. This is not new. The corporation have much to answer for: the old unwritten, unspoken rule that problem families and 'hard cases' should be housed in the West End created a problem of such a size that today it can only be solved by building a new community there.

The general reporting of vandalism and in particular the attention paid to the Mayor's Vandalism Committee amplified the image of the West End as being a centre of 'lawless youth'. In stressing the high level of vandalism in the area, the *Crossley News* was, of course, concentrating on a topic with a strong emotive impact. Throughout the 1960s and early 1970s, vandalism was perhaps the form of adolescent behaviour that the wider society in general found most difficult to come to terms with. Cohen has assessed the almost obligatory use of the terms 'senseless' and 'meaningless' in relationship to vandalism.

> In regard to vandalism, one must understand the nature of the rules which are being broken and the interests or values that are being threatened. Not only are financial costs, aesthetic feelings and physical conventions at stake, but also the perception of vandalism as an inversion of the Puritan ethic which demands that action should be carried out for recognizable utilitarian reasons. It is precisely because such reasons are invisible – nobody 'gains' anything – that vandalism is seen as senseless.[15]

By the early 1970s the West End was seen as a centre for that kind of delinquency which the outside world finds most problematic and mystifying. And this image was maintained and exaggerated by the more general stereotypes being portrayed in the national media of the 'types' of people who become involved in such activities. The national Press and television had produced ready-made stereotypes of such apparently identifiable individuals as the football hooligan, the skinhead and the vandal. And the meanings associated with those 'types' came to be located on the West End. The area was seen to support and produce such activity and as an extension the activity itself was seen as symptomatic of certain pathological characteristics of life in the neighbourhood – in particular the lack of moral education and discipline. The most prevalent response of the Press to the apparently high level of adolescent lawlessness was to 'wage war against the vandals'. The vandals of the West End were seen as a recognisable group of individuals who were fighting

against the good of the community. The image conveyed in
the Press was of a distinct group of young people who had
waged war on society. And the power of the image was made
stronger in that the results of the war were relatively visible.
An attempt, therefore, had to be made to 'combat' them as
well as 'help' them. And it is at this level that the imagery
of the fight against vandalism is congruent with the imagery
suggested above of the 'good of the town'. Vandalism was
seen to be obviously against the good of the town in that
not only was property in general destroyed, but more specifically property belonging to the ratepayers was being
destroyed. The Crossley Press therefore put forward a picture
of all right-thinking people being on one side and the
vandals on the other and this became generalised to the
level of all right-thinking people on one side and the
adolescents of the West End on the other.

PROFESSIONAL WORKERS: THE DELINQUENT
SUBCULTURE OF THE WEST END

Probation officers, social workers, youth workers, police,
clergymen and housing officials all came into regular contact with the Luke Street neighbourhood. And all of these
groups regarded it as a 'problem' area. Indeed, to be a
member of an organisation whose existence is based on
solving problems it is first necessary to define something
as problematic. To fail to do so denies the purpose of one's
existence. Herbert Gans uses the nice term 'external caretakers' to refer to this group of people who live outside
the areas they work in and whose role can be seen as re-
presenting the normative interests of the outside culture.[16]
Into this category of 'external caretakers' he puts among
others the schools and various social-work agencies. Martin
and Fitzpatrick also develop the idea of the 'external care-
taker' specifically in terms of adolescent delinquency:

Basically, external caretakers serve to run things along the
inner frontier for the outside world. Sometimes they are
motivated by the spirit of charity and love; sometimes they

are fulfilling what they see as their professional obligations, sometimes they are just doing a job for which they
get paid. But always they are psychological and cultural
outsiders who are representatives, irrespective of moti-
vation, technique or personal competence, of the dominant
overall society. They are sent in to help to manage, treat or
restrain poor people in trouble or people who are likely
to get into trouble.[17]

There was in fact no single professional definition of the
characteristics or extent of the problem of the West End.
Indeed, the continuing debate over 'what shall we do with
the West End' indicated that there were many sides to the
argument. Allied to this, it is of course necessary to recognise
a distinction between official pronouncements of policy and
approach and the more basic operative definitions that are
adopted in particular situations. But it is important to attempt
to describe some of the themes inherent in the way the 'professionals' set about and viewed their work in relation to
Luke Street . They were often the most obvious indication
to the people of the neighbourhood that their behaviour
and existence was regarded as out of step with the wider
community.

The various professional workers, because of their
relatively detailed knowledge of the West End, did not
regard it as a homogeneous area. Certain sections of it were
regarded as its 'hard core' or centre. With the evacuation
of Cambridge Square, Luke Street and the other Saint streets
came to be thought of as the most prominent of these. For
instance, at a meeting to discuss 'the problems of the West
End' the area's senior social worker claimed that 'The Saint
streets are the heart of it' and Crossley's senior probation
officer stated:

There's some streets in the West End I've never heard of.
But there's some streets that I come into contact with time
and time again . . . We shouldn't keep talking about the
West End. The West End this, the West End that, the Press
keep on talking about the West End but it's not. It's
Cambridge Square and Luke Street.

The police also regarded the West End as providing a
disproportionate amount of their problems. As one police
officer said: 'You've got to agree that the West End is a tough
area and there's quite a few villians down there.' And Luke
Street in particular was singled out as the 'worst street in
Crossley'. One policeman I talked to referred to Luke Street
as 'the sump of Crossley' and another in a formal meeting
stated: 'Luke Street is definitely the worst street in the town.
Definitely. There's no question about it. Luke and Matthew
Street are the worst. Absolutely the worst.'

The most prevalent belief about the neighbourhood held
by these workers was that it was a 'delinquent area'. In spite
of the fact that 'some decent families live down there' it
was believed that delinquent attitudes and values were prevalent, and that many people in the neighbourhood, particularly the young people, were influenced by these.
Everybody was seen to be pulled down to what the professional workers considered the lowest common
denominator. It was believed that delinquent acts and the
values that supported them were a consistent and central
part of the ongoing life of the neighbourhood. The following
remarks made to me at various stages of the research illustrate
the way in which delinquency was regarded by the professionals as a continuing aspect of life in the neighbourhood:

> You've got to be a brave man to live down there and not
> knock things off [Youth Employment Officer].

> The families down there they expect their kids to be put
> on probation. When I go along the street, people say
> things like 'our little Jimmy's nearly ten, he'll soon be
> one of yours'. It seems part of the process of growing up
> down there [Probation Officer].

> The West End conjures up a picture of a delinquent area.
> When you think of the West End that's what you think of
> [Social worker].

Forms of behaviour and, as an extension of this, types
of people were therefore associated with the Luke Street
neighbourhood. And this association was particularly

powerful in the case of 'anti-social' behaviour. Young people were seen to go automatically through a 'delinquent' period as part of the normal process of growing up. The pressures and incentives towards delinquency were seen to be so great that only a boy of remarkable strength could avoid contamination if he lived in or around Luke Street. This association between the individual, his behaviour and the area was perhaps best illustrated by the head naster of one local school who referred to one of his pupils as 'typically Luke Street'.

The professional workers were faced, therefore, with a 'delinquent area'. The majority had fairly well-articulated explanations as to why the situation should be such. These explanations tended to be at two inter-related levels. The first level emphasised the fact that there was 'no environment' in the area. Explanations of this kind centred on the idea that delinquency was a natural way for adolescents to spend their time. It was another case of the devil making work for idle hands. But the blame for the absence of an environment was rarely apportioned. When professional workers did seek to apportion such blame the fault was partly seen as being that of the authorities for not making the necessary facilities available and in a more indirect but perhaps more powerful way as being the fault of the neighbourhood itself for not impressing upon its young people the benefits of 'constructive' activity. There was 'no environment' because the parents had failed to provide one.

The second level of explanation emphasised the role of the family more directly. Families in that particular section of the West End were regarded by the professionals as having a 'low functioning level' and it was believed that there was a 'lack of parental discipline'. A local youth leader told me: 'What I'm doing in three hours is ruined as soon as they go home. The parents aren't in. They're allowed to roam about, do what they want in the house.' And allied to this explanation of the family as the root cause of delinquent values was what could be called the 'famous families' theme. The West End was seen to contain a group of notorious families – what was referred to by a probation officer as a 'sedimental' group – which was well known to all local authority departments as being a constant problem. And it was believed that there were in the area some families which were 'entirely criminal in their history'.

The kind of solutions that were envisaged for the problem of delinquency in the area were of a general nature but had their origin in the belief that the family and the community would have to function at a more effective level if the values of the young people were to be changed. The professional workers considered that they were dealing with a 'delinquent subculture' and believed that the only way to combat it was to go to its root causes. These were perceived to be hidden somewhere in the depths of the 'lack of community' and 'lack of a decent family environment' rather than the whole complex of disadvantages which the local boys had grown up with. Delinquency was seen, therefore, to be the most important indication of some of the key facts about the neighbourhood. What was regarded as the high level of delinquency was taken to stem from the low level of family and community functioning. And it was through delinquency that the neighbourhood came to be categorised as a bad one. The end product of this was again to see the individuals of the neighbourhood in homogeneous and consistent terms as having values which were distinct from their wider community.

The continued attention of professional workers to the West End of Crossley with the intention of cutting down delinquency therefore played its part in creating an image both inside and outside the area of a section of the town which was more and more cut off from conventional society. Possibly the most accurate definition of a problem area is that a lot of professional trouble workers come into contact with it. The great number of such workers who were in evidence in and around Luke Street were there in the attempt to alleviate such individual problems. And in this way they were, of course, occasionally successful. But in doing this, they tended to work on a basic conception of a community whose roots in some strange way were pathological. They thus based much of their work on a straightforward theory of social contamination. If the individual could be drawn away from the contaminating influences then success had been achieved. Therefore, although they were 'concerned' about the problems they faced in the neighbourhood, they were concerned primarily at an individual level. And by individualising the conditions that they came across, they failed to take account of the processes by which the neighbourhood had come to be like it was. The lack of concern that was shown by the professional workers over the corporation housing policies when details of these were published was an indication of their failure to recognise the process that had led to the situation. It is possible to argue, therefore, that the continuing 'concern' in professional circles about the 'problem' of the West End and the continuing conception of it in pathological terms played a significant part in stereotyping the neighbourhood and making it appear further and further from what was regarded as normal social circumstances. One only has to imagine the feelings of a mother in court being told that she is bringing her family up in a 'highly delinquent area' to guess at the implications of this kind of professional stereo-typing.[18]

'BEHAVIOUR DOWN THERE'

The difficulties and ambiguities inherent in the analysis of public stereotypes have been noted. But it is possible to suggest some tentative conclusions concerning the way in which adolescence in the West End and Luke Street was regarded. The area was seen as a 'problem area', one which housed 'problem' families and was seen as the focus of a number of the town's major problems and the location in which those problems took their most extreme form. The attention paid in both the Press and professional circles to 'lawless youth' in the area produced an over-riding perspective of the existence of groups which were in a sense apart from the conventional society and beyond the realms of normal experience. And the dominant perception was the danger of the behaviour of these groups spilling over into other areas. Except for the occasional acknowledgement of the number of 'decent people' who were living there the overall impression was of an homogeneous group of people who lived 'down there' and whose problems and way of life were distinct.[19] It was believed that such was the strength of local values and standards that even those families who tried to maintain a good way of life were likely to be contaminated and their levels of existence dragged down. Everybody in the West End, and more particularly the people of its 'hard core', were thought to be operating at the level of the lowest common denominator. And that lowest common denominator was symbolised by delinquent activity.

By the early 1970s the West End of Crossley had evoked a degree of what has been referred to as moral panic. But in this case, the panic was not so much related to a style but to a whole area. And this moral panic led to the high degree of ambivalence shown towards the area. On the one hand, outsiders wanted to fight against the behaviour of the young people of the area; on the other hand, they wanted to help them raise their standards. But the end result of both these ambitions was that the stereotyped reputation of the West End as a centre of 'lawless youth' was extended. And this, it can be argued, played a significant part in amplifying the belief that the area was associated with 'trouble' and thus played a part in continuing such 'trouble' and increased the difficulties of the adolescents growing up in the area. I am not of course arguing that the area did not support what was by any standards a high rate of officially recognised delinquent activity. The data presented in the previous chapter would make such a contention implausible. What I am arguing is that this form of behaviour was exaggerated in the external perceptions of the area to produce a stereotypical picture of a consistently delinquent group of people.

5

CASEY'S: SOME INTRODUCTORY SKETCHES

I dunno whether you'd call it the worst pub or the best pub in town. It depends on what you mean. Me – I'd call it the worst pub with the best people in it.

Jimmy

So far I have examined external definitions of life in Luke Street. The housing reports, official delinquency statistics and Press stories were the formal indications of what other people thought and did about the neighbourhood. I want now to change the focus and look at what goes on inside Luke Street. My intention in the next five chapters is to analyse delinquency when and where it happens. But before I can deal specifically with delinquent activity in Luke Street it is necessary to describe the social context in which it occurs. That is the purpose of this chapter.

What follows in the next chapters is based on my observations, interactions and conversations in Luke Street. I was involved for eighteen months in the fieldwork for this study and during that period was in direct contact with the people of the area.[1] My time was spent 'hanging around' in the neighbourhood and more particularly in Casey's pub on the corner of Matthew Street and the Dock Road. Besides this I have maintained contact with the area for a further two years during which time I have been able to test out and develop ideas about the neighbourhood in conversation with some of the people who live there. The research approach could be referred to therefore as participant observation and I want at this stage to make several introductory points about this approach.

First the demands made in academic sociology to 'appreciate' the world of the deviant have produced studies in recent years the effects of which are questionable. Being over-concerned to present the 'colour' of their subjects' lives they have produced pictures of groups of people who appear to be far removed from the experience of the majority. In doing this they have been guilty of increasing the apparent gulf between the particular group and the wider society. Indeed the very mechanics of writing 'appreciative' sociology plays a part in this. Having words as their only data many studies adopt the format of close sociological reasoning interspersed with illustrative 'quotes' from their subjects. And in this format the quotes, full of their 'fucks' and local idiom, stand in stark contrast to the organised style of the sociologist. The world of the expert and the person he is expert about seem further apart than ever.

Secondly although the focus of this study is adolescent delinquency it proved impossible both in conducting the study and in writing it to concentrate solely on the boys of the neighbourhood. The problem facing the researcher who goes into a total situation rather than abstracting people out of it is that everything appears related to everything else. In Luke Street it seemed impossible to isolate either individual groups or different aspects of the neighbourhood for separate analysis. The boys' 'delinquent' behaviour was interwoven into the ongoing life of the neighbourhood. In my discussion of their position I have tried, therefore, not only to recognise the continuity between their 'delinquent' and 'non-delinquent' worlds, but also to see them in the context of the neighbourhood of which they were a part and in which they had grown up.

Finally in conducting a study as this the researcher is forced into the position of attaching his own abstracted interpretations to the life he sees around him. He is forced to be selective both in what he observes and in what he presents as his final analysis. There is no guarantee that another person in the same circumstances would observe the same events, have the same conversations and leave with the same impressions. Where one sees hostility another may only see indifference and where one sees humour another may only see resentment. This is, of course, the major weakness of studies which adopt a basically observational approach. Even more so than in other areas of sociological enquiry the reader has to take the writer's word for it. But this basic weakness is matched by an advantage. By simply 'hanging around' the researcher can gain insights into fundamental aspects of life in individual neighbourhoods.

These then are points to keep in mind when approaching any study based solely or partly on participant observation. I want now to paint some introductory and tentative sketches of life in Luke Street. To do this I shall concentrate on Casey's for the following reasons:

(i) Casey's is the focal point of the neighbourhood. Anything that goes on in Luke Street is likely to be known about and talked about in Casey's. Conversations in Casey's offer a commentary on day-to-day life in the neighbourhood.

(ii) Casey's operates as a meeting point for all groups in the neighbourhood from the youngest to the oldest and provides insights into the way in which the different age and sex groupings interact and more generally into the way in which relationships are managed in Luke Street.

(iii) Casey's operates as a socialising institution for the young people of the neighbourhood – particularly the male adolescents. It is here that they learn about adult life and how to deal with it.

(iv) Casey's is an intensely local pub. No strangers are likely to stop on the main road for a drink. In fact the commuters who drive past Casey's on the Dock Road are unlikely to realise that it is a public house at all. For most of the time I was in the area there was no brewer's sign hanging outside and all the windows had been blocked up and painted black. Because it is a very local pub it shows how the Luke Street people deal with the outside world and how they attempt to come to terms with and counteract the way in which the outside world defines them.

(v) The majority of the delinquent incidents described in this study occurred within a twenty-yard radius of the main door of Casey's.

In concentrating on Casey's therefore I am not only setting the scene, I am also beginning to offer an analysis of the social life of Luke Street.

One further introductory point needs to be made. The information for this chapter is based fairly heavily on my friendship with a man called Jimmy Roberts. This is both because I have used his words to describe and explain what is happening in Casey's and more directly because I was with him a lot of the time I was there and got to know his circle of friends. I am quite prepared to admit that my perceptions about the social world of Casey's may be influenced by the way in which Jimmy himself perceived it. This is an unavoidable danger faced by the researcher who does not try to keep a respectable distance from his 'subjects'. But this danger was balanced by the advantage of a relatively easy introduction to the daily life of Casey's that my friendship with Jimmy allowed me. The friendship was of value not only because Jimmy knew literally 'almost everybody' who used the bar but also because he had a sensitive and articulate perception of the social world in which he found himself. Because of this I should perhaps briefly introduce him at this stage. He is an unmarried man in his early thirties and for the majority of my time in the neighbourhood was unemployed. But like a lot of the men who drink regularly in Casey's he has had a fairly varied life and has spent some time at sea. More recently he had worked for differing periods on building sites. Jimmy is characterised by his verbal ability and his willingness to do 'anything for anybody'.

I met Jimmy and got talking to him on one of my first visits to Casey's. It was a Friday night and he was going round the bar with 'spot-the-ball' cards in aid of the Casey's football team. I talked to him briefly while he was doing this and later after closing time talked to him on the corner. He was interested in the idea of research although he 'couldn't see the point of it'. The friendship developed in the following weeks and I became a regular companion of his.

THE PLACE

From the outside there is little unusual about Casey's. It is a square functional building built sometime at the end of the last century. It started life as a small hotel catering for the commercial travellers and businessmen whose affairs brought them to the newly expanded dock town. In its time it would have been a respectable pub sharing in a modest way in the prosperity of the town. The 'dangerous classes' of that period would have lived some way away. But now what former glory it had has faded. As a result of its age, the decline of the town and recent housing and industrial development in its immediate surroundings, the pub has changed into a physically depressing corner pub in a physically depressing area. The term 'hotel' has long since been discarded and the pub is known locally after a land-lord of distant memory – Casey. Outside, the walls of the pub are covered in black grime, the result of half a century of exposure to dockland dirt. A few snatches of graffiti complete the picture – 'Luke Street rule' and the ubiquitous names, Frankie, Rappo, Lombo. Inside, the initial impression is equally depressing. Cigarette smoke has stained the walls and there is little in the way of decoration. A darts score-board, some postcards stuck up behind the bar, a poster brought back from a trip some years ago to swinging London. The furniture is functional and equally depressing – dark polished tables and benches screwed to the floor.

But what Casey's lacks in physical attraction it makes up in reputation. It has all the connotations of being a hard pub in a hard area. Conversations with people who had lived in the Saints streets since the early 1950s and regretted the changes that had taken place there linked the decline of Casey's directly with the decline of the area. Up until 1960 they would go into Casey's for an occasional drink, now they 'wouldn't go near the place'.

AGE AND SEX GROUPINGS IN CASEY'S

Casey's offers something for everybody. To the men of the neighbourhood it is a place where they can go for a drink before their tea and then return to for some more serious drinking later in the evening. It is also an opportunity to 'get away from home'. Luke Street accommodation is poor and crowded. Casey's offers a refuge from the stresses of family living in such conditions. When the men go into Casey's they take it easy and family responsibilities will not intrude on their enjoyment. They can drink, play darts and talk. Talk about what's happened at work and in the street. Talk about what the boss said to someone. He's a cunt him. Talk about what the corporation haven't done. Wankers driving big Rovers and not deserving a penny. Talk about the police. Bastards. Never met a decent one. But most of all talking about sport.

And if you're less inclined to gregariousness you can stand at the bar watching the colour television which offers a continuous backdrop to conversations. Alternatively you can just sit and drink, bothering nobody and nobody bothering you. If you live in Luke Street you don't need an excuse to go into Casey's. 'Going in for a drink' is a good enough explanation.

To the women in Luke Street Casey's offers a less continuous refuge and even here they cannot entirely escape the responsibilities and pressures that their families impose on them. Typically they will only come in at weekends. For the women Casey's is an indication that they're not going to sit at home night after night with the kids and that they want their nights out as well. And on these occasions they will sit at a table with other women separate and distinct from their menfolk. It is not unusual for a Luke Street man to arrive in Casey's with his wife, buy her a drink and then for both to separate for the evening to friends of their own sex. At closing time they will join up again for the walk home. For the women who come into Casey's the evening is an 'occasion' rather than a regular part of the daily round. And because it is an occasion they will anticipate it, and be excited by it. It is perhaps their one night out of the week and they are going to make the most of it. They will dress up smart for their night out. Smoking No. 6s, drinking port and lemonade and rum and black. Extracting all the enjoyment that Casey's can give them. Making the best of life in Luke Street. Talking interspersed with laughter. Somebody had said something and what she said back. Sharing a joke at the end of the week. Occasionally children will peer in the door – they're told to go back home: give your mother a few minutes peace.

Casey's is also the main meeting place for the adolescents of the area. There are no cafes or amusement arcades in the vicinity of Luke Street. Thus Casey's offers a place to hang about. The 'hard' reputation of Casey's, the stories that are still told of incidents there five or ten years ago, are positive incentives to be there and to be associated with Casey's. But the local lads are really just neophytes in a world of job insecurity, bad housing and not enough money. By coming into contact with the men in Casey's the lads are seeing a course for themselves in life. They're learning to accept that life isn't going to offer you much but what it does offer you'll take. No one will stand in the way of what pleasure there is. Casey's is where you learn that. Unemployment. The man at job shop said they'd be lucky if they got anything at the moment. Better make the most of it. Don't want to move away. Luke Street's all they know. Somebody said join the Army. Came to talk at school. Travel, sport. Fuck that.

They're wearing the same denims they wear all the time. No money for best clothes. Just full-time denims. Close-cropped hair, denim jackets, denim jeans and big boots. Most of the boots are nothing special but some of them are Dr Marten's.

The adolescent girls' attraction to Casey's is more limited. The local girls rarely go there because the pub is primarily a male preserve and also because the attraction of the town dance halls is greater. In contrast to the dance halls the ethos of Casey's militates against pairing off. They want to develop a relationship which has elements of permanency. The tension and contradiction between the male and female view of the potential Luke Street heterosexual relationships is nicely summed up for me by a chance remark made by one of the lads: 'Around here you've only got to go and screw a girl and they'll be saying you're going out with her.' The rule at least in the eyes of his colleagues is to avoid being tied down.

For this reason the girls will look elsewhere for steady relationships. And in any case a boyfriend outside the West

End gives the possibility of moving right away from the area. Already some are beginning to anticipate the role of being wife and mother and are ambitious to fulfil these roles away from Luke Street.

Thus pairing relationships between a local lad and girl are rare. The term 'courting' in Luke Street is synonymous with spending one's leisure time away from the area.

EXPECTATION, ANTICIPATION AND BEING A CASEY'S REGULAR

The above are surface sketches of Casey's. But underneath the surface world are a set of ties and obligations. A world of anticipations and expectations. Anticipating, expecting, knowing is part of being a Casey's regular. Little things happen in Casey's that the outsider wouldn't pick up. Two miniature whisky bottles left on the window still. A sign that Harry's been in – he always brings his own miniatures and leaves them after him. Sure sign he's been in. Funny business though taking your own whisky into a pub. Other anticipations. People who don't get on with each other and never have. Wouldn't expect them to notice each other when they go into Casey's. Studied avoidance. Never speak to the cunt – have never got on with him.

Other things particular to the time of day or day of week. Friday dinner-time, for example, three men come into the bar dressed in suits. Very smart, look as if they're on their holidays. Sit down at a table with their pints. To the outsider just three working men smartly dressed for some reason. To Casey's regulars their presence is a sign it's Friday. They work on the bins and always go to work smartly on a Friday. A continuing joke. Nobody works on a Friday. Fuck the bins on Friday.

Also rumours and tensions in Casey's. Somebody's going to get smashed if they keep on like that. I'm warning them, I'll smash them. And there's a private world of experts in Casey's. If you're known you can get help with most things. Local experts in the NAB, work difficulties, what to do if you're picked up by the police. Wait five minutes and have a word with so and so, he should be in soon.

And the stories about Casey's, the telling and knowing of which marks you as a regular. Stories like the bar staying open Christmas Eve afternoon so that knocked-off presents could be distributed. Stories like the time the landlady invited her woman friends from Luke Street in for drinking sessions after closing time and all the Luke Street men banging on the windows 'wanting their rough'. Stories about great celebrations after the local team had won the league. Stories like the night the police came in searching for somebody and he was lying under one of the benches while everyone was crowding to sit on it and so keep him from view.

THE MALE WORLD

Casey's is a male place. Women come to Casey's but they do so in the knowledge that they are entering a male world. And when they enter that male world they have to keep to its ways. If you as a woman consider yourself a cut above the rest, if you keep yourself to yourself, then you don't go into Casey's. Women in Casey's have to accept the male talk, the male jokes and the male's wanting to be with other males. Sit down at a corner table and let the men get on with enjoying themselves.

It is difficult to define what the maleness of Casey's is. Dirty jokes? But they have to be funny as well as dirty – if they're just plain dirty people'll soon get bored. Talking about the world of work. Which ships are in, whose working on what. Talking about enjoyment and leisure, the Friday afternoons they've spent and will spend down at one of the clubs in town where there's an old stripper who does a turn with a Newcastle Brown bottle. Talking about who said what and who'd had what to drink up in the back bar of the Baltic Fleet last Sunday. Talking about doing a bit on the side – foreigners. Where you can get some copper piping cheap.

WORK

The men who live in Luke Street and who drink in Casey's live in a world characterised by fluidity and irregularity of work. Some of them have been to sea early in their lives, so this pattern of irregularity has had an early grounding. But on-shore the main employers are the docks and ship-yards – industries which have traditionally subjected their work-forces to irregular and uncertain employment. And those who are employed directly on the dock are fighting the possibility of redundancy from the increasing use of containerised shipping. Even those who work outside these two mainstay industries are subject to the vagaries of uncertain employment. For instance in the late 1960s a new motorway was constructed running to within a mile of Luke Street. For several years this offered unskilled work which some of the younger men of Luke Street took up. The money was good – even in those days fifty or sixty pounds a week in-cluding overtime. But by the early 1970s this work had come to an end and the men who had worked on it were back to the employment exchange. From £60 a week back to £10 a week for a single man. Periods of good money followed by a return to the weekly D.H.S.S. giro. Periods when you've got enough money to spend ten or fifteen pounds a week on your own enjoyment followed by times when you've hardly got that much to feed your family.

This uncertainty leads to a number of things. First it leads to a philosophy to live now, to enjoy yourself while you can. The realities of life in Luke Street are not conducive to a philosophy of deferred gratification. There is a sense of fatalism and making the best of life. This philosophy is hinted at by common statements in Casey's: 'that's the way it goes', 'you've got to learn to live with your ulcers'. Secondly it leads to a situation in which you don't look down your nose at the bloke with nothing – you might be next. Thirdly it leads to helping out – seeing somebody right for a couple of weeks. Finally, the irregular employment leads to 'making a few bob'. 'Making a few bob' has two connotations. First it can refer to making money over and above one's wages or D.H.S.S. benefits by doing small 'one-off' jobs for other people or by taking on a regular part-time job such as that of a barman. This meaning of 'making a few bob' was particularly relevant for those men who were out of work in Casey's. Secondly the expression could have more directly illegal connotations, in which case it could refer to a variety of activities. For instance the person who 'stripped' an empty corporation house and sold the copper piping downtown at the going price of about £15 was 'making a few bob'.

Apart from those who are in more or less regular employment there is a small group of long-term unemployed who use the pub. People who've been out of work for five or ten years. Men in their forties and fifties. Battered down by trying to keep on living. A drink in Casey's is one of the few things that makes life worth living. And a few of them are seriously affected by the drink – 'cases and a half' in local terminology.

HARDNESS

Casey's is a 'hard' pub. An accurate picture of this can be given by an examination of some of the words used in Casey's to describe the behaviour and 'attitude' of individuals. The list of words that follows is not anything as definite as a system of role–types by which the 'hard culture' of Casey's can be understood. Rather they are words used to either positively or negatively evaluate the behaviour of other people and they thus operate as powerful checks on behaviour (+ = positively evaluated, − = negatively evaluated):

Divvi (−)   Someone who is 'soft'. A 'divvi' lacks the necessary ability and inclination for both physical and verbal aggression. He is not sophisticated in the ways of the world and other people will take advantage of him.

Gobshite (−)   Somebody who is 'all talk': literally somebody from whose mouth shit(e) comes. His 'talk' is not based on accurate knowledge or acceptable attitudes, nor is it backed up by action or the possibility of action. The word can also have the connotation of someone who tries too hard and in too conspicuous a verbal fashion to affirm the values of the group. [2]

Poser (−)   This is synonymous with someone who is regarded

as being 'stuck up'. A poser is a person who 'tries to make
out that he's better than everyone else'. By what he says and
how he behaves, he indicates that he is trying to move away
from the values of the group.

Hard case (+) A person who can handle himself both
verbally and physically but is undemonstrative. Nobody can
take advantage of the hard case and most people are a little
wary of him. Although he typically does not initiate an
aggressive encounter, he can look after himself and turn
it to his advantage when he is involved in one. He finishes
rather than starts arguments. Nobody 'makes a cunt' out of
him.

Mad fucker (+) People are wary of the mad fucker but also
respect him. His behaviour is characterised by its extrovert
character and also its unpredictability. He has physical and
verbal ability although he may be regarded as a 'bit of
a nut'. He is a hard case but unlike the hard case will
have a go at anybody. Whereas the hard case is typically
undemonstrative the mad fucker lets everybody know what
he's thinking. He is always in the middle of things and
is an innovator. There is considerable humour associated
with his style.

Comedian (+) Individual with incisive wit and ability at
repartee. Takes life as it comes. Exaggerates values of the
group through humour.

These words, and others less frequently used, accurately
indicate the extremes of either positively or negatively
evaluated behaviour of the male culture of Casey's. From
them it can be suggested that the attributes which are positively
evaluated are the ability to look after oneself both physically
and verbally and also the ability not to be taken advantage
of. But obviously the majority of men in Casey's could not
be described directly in these terms. Between either the
positively or negatively evaluated extremes were the majority
of men who shared similar interests and who if pushed could
'look after themselves', but whose behaviour did not evoke

either the respect or condemnation of words such as 'gobshite' or 'hard case'. Also of course, one could be regarded as a 'hard case' by simply acquitting oneself in such a way in one instance. But an analysis of these words in common currency in Casey's can offer guidelines for understanding the cultural norms to be found in the pub and the social control mechanisms used to achieve them. An understanding of the meanings attached to these words also indicates the way in which the male culture of Casey's encompassed people of different age groups. For instance the condemnation of a 'poser' was just as powerful coming from a forty-five-year-old man as it was from an eighteen year old. And just as there were 'hard cases' in their late teens, so also were there 'hard cases' in their forties. Although actual 'hard' behaviour could take a different form in two people of different ages the 'attitude' underlying that hardness and the way in which it was reacted to was common to both.

HUMOUR

The humour of Casey's also gives leads to the nature of the male culture. This is Merseyside and people on Merseyside have a way with words. Thus the woman approaching forty is 'an old boiler' and the Jim Reeves song is changed to

I care not what the U. A. B. may say or do,
I know my claims will always come true.

It is of course almost impossible to analyse humour. The fact that it depicts the untypical and highlights the strange makes each piece of humour in a sense unique. But one necessity for humorous interchange is that both the teller and the listener adhere to the same set of ideas and perceptions about certain social situations.

Humour in Luke Street is highly localised and based on people and events in the neighbourhood. In spite of the difficulties of life in Luke Street the local people could 'see the funny side of things' and a rich vein of humour was associated with the theme of 'strange things happen in

Luke Street', and the unpredictability of behaviour. I noted two examples of this kind of humour in my fieldnotes: 'Up in — Road they call them [that is, children] toddlers, down here [in Luke Street] they call them little bastards'; 'having roses in Luke Street is like seeing an army corporal in knickers.'[3] Apart from specific remarks and conversations indicative of an underlying belief that 'anything can happen in Luke Street' it soon became apparent that there was sometimes a more general reaction of humour to the various 'goings on' in the street. It is hard to indicate the exact nature of this reaction, but the way in which people made remarks such as 'they're buggers around here', 'there's some right comedians down here, aren't there' or 'it must be a real education coming down here' indicated its existence.

Also this humour was indicated in snatches of conversation. The following short exchange between a Casey's regular and a policeman outside the local court indicates this:

Policeman I see you've started painting that house of yours.
Johnnie Yes, but I've got to buy some more paint.
Policeman Buy?
Johnnie Yes, you don't rob around our way!

There is also a more general reaction of humour to the initiatives of the police. Occasionally police officers would come into Casey's either following up a specific incident or hoping to obtain general information. The following abstract from my fieldnotes describes such a situation early one evening in Casey's:

About seven o'clock this evening I was sitting in the main bar of Casey's with Eric. He pointed out to me that a plain clothes policeman was standing at the bar. Several minutes later another one came into the bar and ordered a drink but did not say anything to his companion. Through the looks and glances that were circulating in the bar everybody knew they were police. There was no need to say anything. Eric told me that there had been one in just after opening time as well. Considerable humour is attached to the police coming into Casey's, and it's generally believed that 'you can tell them a mile off'. One of the clearest indications is that plain clothes police are always believed to wear their blue duty shirts because they are 'too tight' to buy ordinary ones.

And it's not just the men who exhibit this humour and way with words. Thus one evening I was in the home of Mrs M. when a local councillor came to visit. Mrs M. was being very polite and telling her what a good job she was doing and how everybody liked her. After the councillor had left she burst out laughing and told me: 'Silly old bugger. You got to act a bit soft with them. Give them a bit of sugar.'

Related to the humour about the perceived abnormality of Luke Street was the form of humour that was more directly associated with the external label of the neighbourhood. People in Luke Street were well aware of what outsiders thought of them, and their reaction of frustrated resentment supported a particular kind of humour. The following abstract from my fieldnotes illustrates this point:

Tonight I was talking to Jimmy in Casey's and we got on to talking about the different streets in the area. Jimmy got out a piece of paper and started drawing a diagram of the Luke Street neighbourhood and putting down where every family lived. He then started putting down either the letters L.A. (= law abiding) or L.B. (= law breaking) by each family. First of all he went down the Luke Street names and it worked out at far more L.B.s on the dock side than on the other. From this Jimmy concluded that in Luke Street there was a 'misfits side' and a 'non-misfits side'. He then went on to put down the families living on the Dock Road. These were all designated as L.B.s except for a few old age pensioners. While we were doing this a friend of Jimmy's joined in the conversation with us. Jimmy had put him down as L.A. but he strongly resented this and laughingly referred to himself as an L.B.

The 'stories' of the neighbourhood also tended to focus on the theme of the externally perceived abnormality of the area. An example of such a story was that the Casey's football team were about to win the Sunday league and because the cup was likely to spend a year in the West End the league organisers had had it insured for £200. Another story was that of the local lady who sold her corporation bath to a scrap dealer and then went to the corporation and told them that 'the vandals have had my bath' and was given another one. Closely allied to the stories that circulated in the area were the beliefs about certain 'characters' in the neighbourhood who seemed to be well known because they supported a general theme of 'strange things happen in Luke Street'. These characters could be of any age and included Mr M. who was reputed to keep a large padlock on his gas meter and carry the key on his belt, Mr S. who was reputed to have a lead mine in his garden – corporation lead, and R. who was nine and regarded as having already forgotten more about delinquency than most people knew. A current joke was that he would give up crime at ten – the age of criminal responsibility.

TALKING SPORT

Talking sport and playing sport is central to the male culture of Casey's. Sport is something that is talked about, argued about, shouted about. Talking sport is institutionalised argument in which anyone can take part. The ability to talk sport is the membership credential to the social world of Casey's. It gives the opportunity for everybody to contribute. Everybody can have opinions and you're as likely to be right as the next man. It's having opinions that's important. Sport offers a sense of belonging. To quote Jimmy:

> Sport is the main function in Casey's. Sport's more important in Casey's than in most pubs. Everything we talk about is geared to sport, horse-racing, cards. I've only known sports. You feel safe and confident in talking about sport because you know you're on an equal basis with them and in some cases better . . . That's basically what Casey's is about – sport.

And in Casey's there were experts in each particular sport. Again to quote Jimmy:

> Big Dave is the expert on fishing and boxing . . . you know, like if you have an argument over a fish, well Dave can give you all the answers. How many teeth its got . . . how much it weighs: And Paddy's the Irish encyclopedia on darts.

Some of the Casey's regulars carried on dialogues entirely in relation to sport and would make little other conversation. As the following abstract from my fieldnotes illustrates, this was entirely accepted:

> I was standing with Jimmy at the bus stop at about 3.30 in the afternoon waiting to go down town. We had spent the dinner-time in Casey's. A Casey's regular came up to us. Without saying anything else he said 'Who was the heavy-weight champion in 1923?' Jimmy gave him the answer. They then went through the dates of all the heavyweight boxing champions of that period and he walked off. This was the entire conversation. There was no hullo and no goodbye.

Not only is sport central to the conversation culture of Casey's. It is also central to the social organisation of the pub. Casey's runs two darts teams with regular weekly matches in the league. Darts night is the big night in Casey's. The bar will be more crowded than at any other time in the week. There's not only the regulars but the away darts team and their supporters. On darts night there will be approaching seventy people in the bar. Everyone will be straining to see what's happening. There will be shouts for silence before each throw and clapping afterwards if it's deserved. It's almost all over-formal. Everyone is enjoying acting for the big occasion. Everyone, including the lads, is subdued during the match – the joking is saved for afterwards.

Even more important for the social organisation of Casey's is the local football team. It is run from Casey's and

although people who don't live in Luke Street play in it,
it is seen as the football team of the Luke Street neighbourhood. The team is efficiently run and successful. It plays
in the town's Sunday League and a lot of the Casey's regulars
will go out and support it on the Sunday morning and
then back into Casey's for a dinner-time drink.

The team is run by a local committee with its own manager,
trainer and treasurer. The manager is Robbie, an out-of-work
Luke Street father, and the trainer is Jimmy himself. Robbie
was rarely the most vocal in the various formal and informal
meetings related to the football team but it was his word
that was all important to the running of the team. Jimmy
described him as the 'main man – our governing body'.

One very important point about the local football team
is that it spans the age range of Casey's. It brings the elder
males and the lads into direct contact. The men manage,
advise and control. The younger men and the lads play.
Thus a social system exists which cuts across the age groups
in Luke Street. The same ambitions and excitements are
shared. Rappo for instance, whom we get to know better in
the next chapter, is a very good footballer – a bit wild perhaps
but a good footballer and a useful asset to the team.

The lads accept the authority of the elder men who run
the team. None of the antagonisms here. And Jimmy takes
a pride in 'bringing on' the young players. His policy is to
let them have a go in the big matches:

> We make a little bit of an effort 'cause it's all the young
> lads who go into Casey's. We make a bit of an effort to
> bring them into the team. The team runs around Casey's.
> It's not like a team really . . . it may sound a bit far
> fetched but it's more like a way of life.

A NOTE ON SUBCULTURES

The research worker in delinquency is typically aware of
one fact on entering an area such as Luke Street – that it
provides the adult and juvenile courts with a disproportionate
amount of their clientele. In seeking the reason for this fact
he sets out to analyse what he supposes to be the 'culture'

of the neighbourhood in the belief that there must be something consistently 'abnormal' about a culture which could produce such a situation. There is a tendency to see delinquent behaviour as consistent over a period of time, as the result of consistent pressures, and as somehow a uniform and observable phenomenon. The researcher tends to think that all the coversations he has and all the interactions he witnesses in a neighbourhood such as Luke Street will support a central theme of deviant behaviour. It is almost as if he expects to find the delinquent subculture hanging a foot above every bar he goes into. It is, therefore, a little disconcerting to find that the vast majority of things that are said to him and the vast majority of events that he witnesses are entirely 'conventional' in terms of the wider community. In this disheartening fact lies the major difficulty he has to come to terms with. He has to learn literally to 'take life as it comes'.

The concept of subculture has been increasingly questioned in recent years. Burgess for instance as early as 1946 warned against the over-estimation of the break between the delinquent subculture and the wider society: 'Some, especially those who had comparatively little first-hand research contact with the delinquency world came to view the delinquency subculture as a whole and complete social system in itself in a self-sustaining society at war with society – a more or less autonomous social entity and reality.'[4] And Valentine has argued against the 'intellectual fad of attributing a subculture to almost any social category'.[5]

It is necessary then to admit that much of what happened in Casey's was not unique. A social researcher could have gone into other pubs on Merseyside and come away with similar experiences. The people of Casey's inhabited a cultural world which was unintelligible to outsiders. Casey's was just one example of the 'hard' dock pubs on Merseyside catering for an almost entirely local clientele. In a sense what made it special was the fact that the people who went there believed it was special.

The second point to make about Casey's is the essential continuity between the adult and the adolescent male worlds. Different age groups used Casey's and often stayed in their

own distinct groups but the dominant impression is of people
of different ages living in the same cultural world. Thus
the eighteen-year-old boy on the corner whom the outside
world characterises in terms of his age and his 'skinhead'
style, was in a more basic sense simply an illustration of
what being male in the cultural environment of Luke Street
meant. It is of course difficult to give what would usually
be acceptable as sociological evidence for this. But the ease
of contact between members of different age groups, the
similarity of patterns of conversations and the similarity of
the humour that developed gave combined indications of
its existence. More subtly the similarity of personal style
also indicated its existence. It is almost impossible to
illustrate this in words but the following fieldnote abstracts
show something of what I mean about contact between
different age groups in terms of the male culture:

Mr M. who is a man in his late fifties and is now beginning
to go a little deaf was standing at the bar talking to myself
and two boys of about 19. The conversation was a fairly
normal one about sport. It also turned to a discussion of
the police following an incident in the neighbourhood
yesterday. The three of them talked about the unfairness of
the police and expressed their opinions in a similar
fashion. The boys were deferential to the opinion of the
older man. While Mr M. was talking he was occasionally
dropping a match box into his instep and then flicking it
up and catching it.

Mr P. (age approximately 45) was sitting in Casey's at
dinner-time. When I came in he came up to me and said
he got fined £5 this morning. He then proceeded to tell
me why he had been fined (drunk and disorderly). He was
telling everybody who would listen to him. Martin (age
15) came in and Mr P. told him and also got out his
charge sheet for him to see. They laughed about the charge,
Martin being deferential to the older man.

This essential continuity between the adult and adolescent
male worlds was recognised by the men in the bar. Thus

men in their thirties and forties will tell you 'I know what it's like to be a kid around here. I've been in trouble like the rest of them.' More importantly the continuity was indicated by the approach of the lads to the men in Casey's. The lads knew their place when they were in the bar. I rarely came across tension and aggression between adolescence and adult males in the area. The men were the real 'hard' cases. The lads knew that if they stayed in the area it would be only a matter of a few years before they had left the corner and had graduated to the bar. Conversely the men were either amused or bored by the style and activity of the boys. Or more typically they simply saw it as part of the process of growing up in Luke Street. The skinhead style may be different from what it was twenty or thirty years ago but 'there's always been lads like that'. The thirty-five-year-old docker is not going to lose any sleep over the seventeen-year-old boy. I suggest that this is important to remember when bombarded by theories of the 'generation gap' or 'lack of respect for authority' variety to explain behaviour such as is described in the following pages.

6

THE BOYS ON CASEY'S CORNER

Luke Street's had a bad reputation for about eight years.
Loads of families were moved down the West End. They
put all the big families down here. And all the kids
went off their fucking heads together.

Frankie[1]

In no field of sociological enquiry are generalisations more
prevalent than in the analysis and description of the position
of young people. Overall theories are produced to explain
both their conventional and unconventional behaviour. And
many different perspectives have been adopted as to the
motivating factors behind this behaviour. Underlying these
generalised theories has been a surprising lack of research
into local situations. Little attention has been paid to local
differences of tradition, economic organisation and
neighbourhood composition in relation to young people.
The result of this lack of research at a local level has been
first that the tentative findings from one piece of research
have been accorded a general validity often far outreaching
their author's original intentions. Secondly, young people
have been seen to be reacting to general societal conditions
rather than to the local situations through which these
conditions are transmitted. These shortcomings in research
are particularly evident in the case of those adolescents who
occasionally become involved in activity which the wider
society regards as delinquent. In spite of the mass of information on attitudes, family background, personality composition and group structure as they relate to delinquency as
yet relatively little is known about the actual behaviour

which comes to be defined as delinquent. In other words, we know a lot more about adolescent delinquents than we do about adolescent delinquency. There are, of course, some important practical reasons for this lack of research at a local level. Like most forms of behaviour that society regards as problematic delinquency is difficult to observe. The participants themselves cannot understand why anybody should be anxious to witness their behaviour unless for the purpose of sanctioning them, the researcher puts himself into a position of legal risk by being involved in delinquency, and the situations in which such activity takes place are often neither predictable nor congenial. Our knowledge of adolescent delinquency, therefore, may well be more related to the nature of the research task than to the nature of the activity itself.

To counteract some of the generalised writing in the fields of adolescence and delinquency one of the purposes of this book is to describe a local neighbourhood. More specifically it is to suggest the connection between the development and organisation of this neighbourhood and the kinds of daily interaction that it supported. Previous chapters have described the decline of Luke Street, the high rates of official delinquency in the neighbourhood and the image of it as being a 'delinquent' area. Consistent with my approach of using different levels of analysis to describe the production of delinquent behaviour in Luke Street I now therefore change the focus of the study to an essentially ethnographic description and analysis of the position and activities of a group of boys in the area known locally as the 'boys on Casey's corner' or the 'Luke Street boys'. The purpose of the following chapters is not however simply descriptive. The lives of the boys should not be seen in a vacuum but should be seen in the context of the wider problems that faced the neighbourhood.

THE GROUP

The research for this study was undertaken in 1971–3. During that time I came to know well some of the boys who had been brought up in and around the Luke Street neighbour-

hood. I gained initial contact with the boys through working
as an assistant at a local youth club and afterwards became
accepted as a person who was alright to know and who
could be 'trusted'. Much of my research time was thereafter
spent 'hanging about' in Luke Street and drinking in Casey's
ale house.[2] During my period of 'hanging about' I came
to know some twenty-five of the local boys and I have used
interview data from some of this wider group to illustrate
certain general points about adolescent life in Luke Street.
But my contact was more extended with a group of nine
of these boys – the 'boys on Casey's corner' – and it is
primarily on my contact with this smaller group that the
following analysis is based. In relation to this, one crucial
point should be stressed at this stage. This group of nine
boys was not an artificial grouping in the sense that it simply
comprised the individual boys whom a sociologist happened
to come to know. The boys regarded themselves as being
individuals who 'hung about' with each other and local
residents would have known who was being referred to by
the term 'the boys on Casey's corner'.

This group was not however a constant grouping over time
and friendship patterns in Luke Street as elsewhere were not
static; thus in some ways the collective name of the 'boys
on Casey's corner' makes the group appear more homogeneous, more defined and more constant than it was. In
fact the group was composed of small groups or pairs of
friends, and although an individual boy would know all
the others who 'knocked about on the corner' he might only
have close contact with two or three of them. Membership
of the group also had a degree of fluidity because of the
frequency with which boys from the neighbourhood were
sent to various correctional institutions. The common
expression in the neighbourhood of someone being 'away'
which included being at an approved school through to
being in prison, indicated the relatively commonplace nature
of this. Reggy from Luke Street, who was nineteen and had
stopped hanging about on the corner, described the effects
of this fluidity on the group in its most extreme form: 'When
I was young, you'd go away and then you'd come out and
several of your mates would go away. So you weren't with

any of your mates. As one of you got sent home, one of your mates would be put away.'

But the corner offered the boys a definite meeting place and a focus for their activities and they were thus a self-selected group in as much as they had made a choice of place, time and companions. The corner brought them together. The significance of having such a meeting place was indicated by Frankie's elder brother who had also stopped hanging about on the corner: 'They're no worse than anybody else around here. There's lads like that all over this town. The only difference is that down here they've got a place to hang about. A place they all come to.'

SOME BIOGRAPHICAL NOTES

In order that the nine boys on which my analysis is primarily based can be seen in the context of their neighbourhood I now present brief biographical details and notes. I have also included comments on how these boys related with each other.

Rappo Aged nineteen,[3] lives in Luke Street. One of a family of eleven who arrived in the area in 1955. No record of other offenders in the family. Rappo is a well-known figure in and around Luke Street. He is also well-known to the various professional workers who came into contact with the area. Although the Luke Street boys lack the close-knit cohesion of a 'gang', Rappo is their self-styled leader. People inside and outside the neighbourhood refer to 'Rappo and his mob'. Rappo has been involved in a number of delinquent escapades but his position of influence in the group is mainly based on his physical strength, his ability to maintain his reputation without necessarily putting this reputation to the test, and his verbal dexterity. And although Rappo rarely puts his strength to the test his reputation is based on the firm ground that several years earlier he had 'seen off' a powerfully built local man in his late twenties. His quick wit and ability in repartee is evident whenever the group are together and particularly when they are in contact with authority. Rappo in fact has *style* and it is this style that keeps

him one step ahead of the rest. My fieldnotes record two
examples of this. Rappo occasionally walked around with
a rolled umbrella; but this innocent looking umbrella
had in fact been modified – the stem had been sawn off at
the top and filed down into a spike, and the umbrella had
then been reassembled. All Rappo needed to do if he was
in 'trouble' was to pull off the fabric of the umbrella and
he had a dangerous sword. In fact Rappo never to my knowledge actually used this weapon. Another example of
Rappo's style was in the court case when he was finally
sent for Borstal training. All the other boys turned up in
their usual blue denim jackets but Rappo put on a specially
pressed white denim jacket and acquired a pair of dark glasses
for his appearance in the dock.

In most of the daily life of the Luke Street boys Rappo's
influence was not consistently important. Indeed there were
some days and weeks when he failed to 'show' on the corner.
But when all the lads 'came together' Rappo was always
much in evidence and influenced the proceedings.

Frankie Aged seventeen, lives in Luke Street. Unemployed.
One of a family of six who arrived in Luke Street in 1955.
Father sick and long-term unemployed. One elder brother
has criminal record. After leaving school Frankie had a
series of short-lived jobs but by the time I got to know him
he had been unemployed for nearly a year. Frankie is a
powerfully built boy who if the circumstances necessitate
will have a go at anybody. He is an 'original' in that he
suggests things to do and shows a certain flair for 'getting
in situations'. A strong vein of humour runs through his
conversations about himself and his position. Because of his
unpredictability it is accepted that one has to 'go a bit careful
with Frankie'.

Eddy Aged twenty, lives in the Dock Road. Unemployed.
One of a family of eight who arrived in the area in 1970.
One younger brother has criminal record. Eddy, like
Frankie, has had a number of jobs but had been unemployed
for an extended period when I got to know him. He is shorter
and less powerfully built than Frankie but has the same

reputation for being involved in delinquent activity. In a
sense Eddy is the elder statesman of the group in that he
is more articulate than the other boys and has 'been around
more'. He fulfils the role of the theorist of the group in
that he articulates the position in which the boys find themselves and provides some of the logic for the occasions in
which they come into contact with authority.

Lombo   Aged eighteen, lives in the Dock Road. Unemployed.
One of a family of eight who arrived in the area in 1958.
Three brothers also have criminal records. Medium height
but strongly built. Has been involved in a number of
major incidents and has a considerable reputation locally.

Phil   Aged seventeen, Lombo's brother. Has a more regular
work record than Lombo. Has been involved in a number of
incidents. But more restrained than Lombo. Content to take
second place to his brother.

Kenny   Aged sixteen, lives in Dock Road. One of a family of
ten who arrived in area in 1960. Elder brother has number of
convictions. Kenny plans to go away to sea when he is old
enough but is unemployed at the moment. Kenny feels a
little out of his depth with Rappo, Frankie and Eddy and
attempts to compensate for this by an over-elaborate and
often inappropriate display of 'hard' behaviour. But he is
generally popular.

Brown   Aged seventeen. Lives just around the corner from
Luke Street in Cambridge Road. Like the others he has had
an irregular work record and had been unemployed for
some months when I met him. He is a close friend of Eddy
and spends a lot of time with him.

Masso   Aged sixteen. Lives about a quarter of a mile away
from Luke Street but spends most of the daytime and evening
in the Luke Street neighbourhood. Masso was brought up
in Cambridge Square but his family has been rehoused to
a street which he considers 'dead boring – really quiet'. On
leaving school Masso declined to accept a place at the local

technical school because only 'divvies go to tech' and has been unemployed since. He considers that the main reason he cannot get a job is that his school refuses to give him a reference. He is lightly built and like Kenny probably feels a little out of his depth alongside Rappo, Frankie and Eddy.

Mal Aged eighteen, lives in Luke Street. For most of my time in the area Mal had a part-time job. Mal is a member of a family of nine who arrived in the area in 1965. His father, elder brother, second brother and two of his sisters have a record of criminal convictions. Although Mal tries to hang around with the group he is something of an outsider. His unpopularity is linked with the more general unpopularity of his family, the result of numerous incidents of inter-family tension in the street. By the end of my research period Mal had recognised his position and no longer hung about with the group.

The above then are brief notes on the nine 'boys on Casey's corner'. It was also possible to abstract from the criminal records the individual list of offences for seven of these boys. To preserve the anonymity of the individuals concerned I am presenting these seven records of conviction in random order. It should also be noted that these lists of offences include several that were committed after the end of the full-time research period.

Case One	Age 15	Possessing an offensive weapon
	Age 16	Theft
	Age 18	(i) Burglary
		(ii) Theft
	Age 19	Assault police (2 cases)
		Wilful damage
Case Two	Age 17	Attempted burglary
	Age 19	Use threatening behaviour
		Assault police
	Age 21	Burglary
		Going equipped for stealing
	Age 21	Criminal damage

Case Three	Age 15	(i) Theft
		(ii) Burglary with intent
	Age 17	Unauthorised taking of conveyance (rowing boat from docks)
	Age 18	Disorderly behaviour
	Age 18	(i) Threatening behaviour
		(ii) Criminal damage
	Age 20	Criminal damage
	Age 20	(i) Criminal damage
		(ii) Assault occasioning actual bodily harm
		(iii) Use threatening abusive or insulting words

Case Four	Age 12	Robbery with violence
	Age 12	Driving a moped knowing it to have been unlawfully obtained
	Age 13	Receiving
	Age 14	Attempted burglary
	Age 16	Knowingly allow himself to be carried in motor vehicle taken without owner's consent
	Age 17	Found in enclosed garden
	Age 17	(i) Assault occasioning actual bodily harm
		(ii) Assault with intent to resist arrest
		(iii) Wilful damage
	Age 19	Burglary and theft
	Age 19	Criminal damage
	Age 19	Assault (2 cases)

Case Five	Age 13	Receiving
	Age 15	Disorderly behaviour
	Age 15	Common assault (2 cases)
	Age 16	Unauthorised taking of conveyance (rowing boat from docks)
	Age 17	Disorderly behaviour
	Age 17	(i) Assault occasioning actual bodily harm
		(ii) Assault police (3 cases)

Case Five	Age 17	(iii) Wilful damage
	Age 18	Wilful damage
Case Six	Age 14	Burglary and theft
	Age 15	Wilful damage
	Age 16	Grievous bodily harm
	Age 17	(i) Assault occasioning actual bodily harm
		(ii) Theft (2 cases)
	Age 17	Burglary and theft
	Age 17	(i) Drunk and disorderly
		(ii) Criminal damage
	Age 18	Assault police
Case Seven	Age 16	Handling stolen goods
	Age 19	Criminal damage

Apart from the length of some of the above records of official convictions the most striking thing about them is their indication of the types of officially recognised delinquent activity that the boys were involved in. For the neighbourhood generally, as has been shown in Chapter 3, charges for theft were in the majority. But for this particular group of boys charges for delinquency of a non-material nature were in the majority. The records of official delinquency indicate that the seven boys of the nine for whom such records were available had been convicted for twenty-one cases of theft as against forty cases of a non-material nature (e.g. theft offences = 35 per cent). In other words there is an almost exact reversal of the rates for the neighbourhood generally. And my knowledge of the court cases in which the other two members of the group were involved supports this general pattern. Although their delinquent activity therefore took place against a backcloth of more general delinquent behaviour in the neighbourhood, the 'boys on Casey's corner' were primarily involved in cases which could be referred to as 'street offences' (i.e. assault, assault on police, criminal damage, etc.) This alerts us to the possible dangers produced by such theories as those of Cloward and Ohlin[4] which stress particular *general* styles of delinquency for particular neighbourhoods and purport to explain relatively 'pure' types of local delinquent subcultures. There is a necessity to be specific and analyse the delinquent patterns of groups in individual neighbourhoods rather than relying on interpretations based on overall rates. It is also interesting to note that the records of convictions I have included here appear to indicate that most of the boys had started their official delinquent careers with theft offences and then became increasingly involved in charges of a non-material nature.

During my time with the boys there were examples of theft behaviour but this behaviour was characterised by its irregular and *ad hoc* nature. It is important however to indicate certain characteristics of this behaviour and to produce some examples. For instance there were cases of the boys stealing crates of soft drinks from delivery lorries outside Casey's and Casey's itself was subject to at least two break-ins while I was working in Luke Street. Indeed one of the regulars explained to me that the pub offered the local boys an apprenticeship in crime in that 'everybody around here has knocked off Casey's at one time or another'.

Another form of theft which occurred in my time in Luke Street marked a particular adaptation to the local opportunity structure for delinquency. A single line railway track runs alongside the Dock Road on the opposite side to Casey's. This track carries goods from one section of the docks to the other. The majority of goods are carried in large container units but occasionally trains come past Luke Street with open wagons of coal. Twice during my time in Luke Street boys were involved in a routine which involved one of them waiting until the train stopped at the entrance to the docks and then crawling under one of the coal wagons and opening the unloading hatch. The train would then pull off and the contents of the wagon would fall out on to the track. Immediately groups of the local boys would then come out of hiding and collect the coal and spirit it away into the sanctuary of Luke Street.

Such examples of theft were infrequent, but one of the most common forms practised by the boys was what was known locally as 'house-stripping'. Luke Street itself, as is shown in Chapter 2, contained a number of empty houses and the area immediately adjoining it also had a large number of such houses. Cambridge Square was in particular at the time of the beginning of my study almost half empty as people were moved out of it in preparation for its demolition. When one of the local houses or flats in Cambridge Square became empty it was likely that within twenty-four hours the boiler, water tanks and piping would be ripped out. The frequency of this and the problems it caused for the local housing department have been referred to but it is useful to examine the mechanisms of this operation in a little more detail. 'house-stripping' which outsiders and housing officials regarded as an example of adolescent vandalism was indulged in not only by some of the older boys but also by some of the men in the area. When a corporation house was to be vacated this went around the local grapevine. In Casey's people 'kept their ears open' about houses that were to be vacated and the first night that a house was empty a group of either two or three would break in and strip it. The boiler, water tank and piping would be taken downtown the next day to a scrap metal dealer who didn't ask questions. At the time of my study, the proceeds from an average corporation house could produce something between twenty and twenty-five pounds. However the damage caused by this operation could run into hundreds or even thousands of pounds per house and explains the corporation's desire to board up houses immediately they became vacant and for departing tenants to inform them of the exact day and hour they were leaving the property. But such boarding up operations were usually ineffective against the efforts of local house-strippers. House-stripping was therefore a relatively pervasive activity in and around Luke Street and resulted in the high number of 'vandalised' houses. But this vandalism was neither 'senseless' nor 'meaningless'. It was distinctly utilitarian and this can explain why both adults and adolescents were involved in it. This puts into perspective the statement often heard in the neighbourhood: 'it's not the young ones that do all the vandalism around here.'

These then are examples of delinquent activity of a theft nature in which the boys were involved. But the most important events to analyse in terms of their delinquent careers are the incidents on the street and it is to this analysis that I now turn.

PROBLEMS OF EXISTENCE

The boys on Casey's corner faced three specific difficulties related to their position: (i) the lack of a routine of both work and leisure which a regular job could provide; (ii) the lack of money that a regular job could provide; (iii) the restriction in terms of the space allocated to the boys.

As was shown in Chapter 2, Crossley had nearly twice the national average of unemployed workers at the time of this study. And unemployment was particularly severe amongst young people. Although the boys on Casey's corner, except those who had recently left school, had all worked at some stage, they were unemployed for most of the time I knew them. And those who had worked had found their jobs badly paid and unrewarding. When I had the following taped conversation with Lombo he had been unemployed for six weeks. His work record up until then is fairly typical:

Lombo First job was at — which I got right after leaving school. That's right over the road from Casey's.
O.G. What were you doing there?
Lombo I was on the causting, cutting the drums out.
O.G. How long did you stay doing that?
Lombo Three months.
O.G. What made you leave?
Lombo The money. Only £5 a week. Then I went straight away to — making wooden panels. I was there three months and then I packed it in because the pay was no good. Then I went to —. I was a painter there. But I was only there a year and I was made redundant. Then I went to the pie factory. For 3 months. I got the sack for fighting. I was peeling potatoes and he told me to go on to spraying pies. I said I'm not going to do it. He said give me that potato. I said no. He said give it me else I'll smash your head in. I said fuck off and I hit him. He got me the sack.

Webbo and Frannie who used to hang about with the group occasionally had also left their jobs in similar circumstances.

Webbo I'd been working for 6 months in that factory. I suppose if I'm honest I'd been trying to get the sack for the last six weeks. I hit the boss's son when he told me to go a message.

Frannie They gave it me yesterday. The sack. The boss had always been getting at me. He said I'd have to spend the first two days of this week breaking up wood. There were piles of it so I thought fuck that. I'm not doing that, so I didn't turn up on Monday. And yesterday they gave it to me.

But by the time I got to know the boys, jobs had become increasingly difficult to find:

Mal I've got lots of trades but I can't get anything. Nothing. They say you've got to have a trade to get a job. But I can't get one. And it's not because I don't try because I do.

Chas You go a long way for a job. You know like down to —. And when you get there a bloke just says you're too late or they'll let you know. It gets you down.

Rappo The jobs go to all the toffee noses. The likes of us don't get a look in . . .

Frannie What's the good of going. Even references won't get you in a job in this town.

Masso had been unemployed since leaving school six months previously: 'I can't get a job. I've tried but I couldn't get one because the school didn't give me a reference.'

Besides the basic difficulty of there being simply too few jobs available, the boys believed that they suffered from the particular disadvantage of living in the West End. Here, Brown, Eddy and Masso describe how they applied for jobs and then, on giving their address, had been told that the jobs were no longer available:

Brown I've been all over Crossley, everywhere. But I can't get a job.

Eddy They say where you come from . . .
Brown   And you say West End. And they say sorry you can't come.
Masso You can't get nothing around our end.
Eddy I went for a job at —, I said any jobs? They said yes – start tomorrow. Then they ask for particulars and once they see Luke Street or Cambridge Square they say you can't come down here you're too rough, you're a fucking slum-dweller.

Clivo also indicated what was thought to be the difficulty of getting a job with a 'bad' address. 'If you go for a job and you say you live in the West End, they said "have you been in trouble"?' And many of the boys suffered from the further handicap of having been 'inside', and thus having irregular work records. This again jeopardised their position in the job market. Reggy for instance who had been through the whole range of correctional institutions told me:

> The biggest problem is that I go for a job and they say get your cards and come back. Well I do that and I show them the cards and as soon as I give them to them, the cards are blank, so I've got to say where I've been. I can't say I've been out of town. If you've been away that's it. I haven't worked for two years or so, if I take my cards in there's nothing on them. That goes against it. I went to the building site at the bottom of — Street. I went in there and he said 'start on Monday. Bring your cards in.' So Monday, I went in and showed him my cards. And he said where've you been. You haven't got nothing on your cards. So I said I'd been away. Well he never said outright I can't start. He made the excuse – well I don't know if it was an excuse – that I wasn't in the union.

By the time of my contact with the boys, therefore, their employment difficulties had become severe. Most of them had come to recognise the insecurity of employment or at its most extreme the inevitability of unemployment. And in the Luke Street neighbourhood there were plenty of older

men to illustrate that this insecurity was the norm. In Casey's
they could see the unemployed older brother of twenty-five
and the unemployed father of forty-five. And through this
contact with older unemployed men they had come to see
a possible pattern for their own lives. But the boys did not
suffer simply from the general difficulty of finding work.
They came from an area which they believed was discriminated against in the job market and some of them faced
the added difficulties of being unable to find work because
of the time they had spent in correctional institutions. The
cumulative effect of all these factors was that unemployment
had come to be regarded as the norm and a norm that it
was no use fighting against. The longer they were unemployed, the worse things became in as much as they were
caught up in the spiral of no job experience leading to
no job offers. In the competitive market of an employer
being able to be selective they had nothing to offer. The
effects of this were cumulative. The longer they stayed unemployed the less experience of 'job discipline' they were
seen to have and the less willing employers were to take them
on. And underlying all these factors was the recognition
that if they did find work then that work would be mono-
tonous, badly paid and uncongenial. The wisdom of even
looking for work came to be questioned.

Related to the boys' unemployment was their lack of
money. The boys under the age of eighteen received £3.60
per week supplementary benefit. Those over eighteen received
£4.70. Towards the end of my time in Luke Street the rate
of benefit for under-eighteens was increased from £3.60 to
£4.70 a week. Frankie joked about this and referred to it
as 'the rise'. Out of this money an average of £2.00 per
week was given to their families for food and keep, but most
of them increased this when they were given the rise. The
average spending money per week for the boys was thus under
£2.00 per week. Out of this £2.00 some of the boys were
paying off fines at perhaps £1 per week. These rates of benefit
should however be seen within the context of what the boys
were able to earn at work. The difference was not large.
For instance, one of the group before he got the sack had
been earning £6 a week. Out of this he paid his family the

higher sum of £3.00 a week and had to pay 57p for his stamp. This left him £2.43 a week spending money.[5]

The third basic fact of the boys' existence concerns their access to space. They were limited as to where they could go and what they could do. In part this was, of course, the result of their lack of money. But there were other reasons which were specific to the Luke Street neighbourhood. First, as has been shown in Chapter 2, the boys had been brought up in very large families where space in the home had been severely limited. Because of this the street had come to be a natural and not unattractive alternative to the home during childhood and this pattern had continued into middle and late adolescence. But apart from simply being on the street there was nothing to do:

Eddy There's no entertainment around here. Nothing for nobody – if you're on the corner like, you've got nothing to do except play football in the street.
Jacko You can't go fucking nowhere can you?

Added to this it was felt by the boys that simply because of the stereotypes surrounding their address, they were restricted in places where they could go. Although most of the boys were now past the normal age for youth club attendance this limited access to space because of 'what people think of us' was probably at its most extreme in the feeling of resentment about the nearby youth club, a feeling of resentment which again appeared to be linked to the 'tradition' of the previous decade:

Joe You can't get into the – [club] from around here.
Pat If you give an address like Luke Street, they just say they're sorry they haven't got any places. It's the same as everything else if you're from Luke Street you're not on.
Frankie — [club leader] wouldn't let Rappo and me in. You know the fucking place was empty one night. I said to him he's let fucking loads of visitors in. He'd let in loads of visitors in from all over town. You go to any clubs in Crossley and say you're from the West End and they won't let you in.

Eddy When I first came up here from — Street, I went to the club and asked him how much it is. So he said where do you come from. And so I said Dock Road, and he'd say sorry no you can't get in.

The youth leader in question explained this policy to me in the following way in a taped conversation. This excerpt nicely illustrates the way in which he regarded some of the Luke Street boys and what he considered to be the dangers of 'contamination':

Quite a few people didn't really want to come in and enjoy the club. I'll give you an example — [one of the boys on Casey's corner]. He just wanted to come in and create a nuisance. To stir up trouble. I got to the stage where certain people I wouldn't allow in because I knew I'd lose fifty per cent of my members. I used to hear kids saying I'm not coming here if he's coming. Alright, the youth service says the club's open for everybody, but the people who say this aren't running the clubs. I would rather look after the fifty members who are on the balance and keep them on the good side, than bring in a couple who I knew I could do nothing with and neglect my other members and find that they've gone bad. For instance I've got nothing against him personally. I'll have a laugh and a joke with him, but I wouldn't have him in the club . . . I prevent trouble instead of allowing it to start.

These then were the three basic facts of existence, and the way in which they were interpreted, of the boys who came together regularly on Casey's corner. They produced a corresponding set of problems with which the boys had to come to terms in their daily lives. First because they had no work they had very little money to spend. Secondly, because they had no jobs, no money and nowhere to go they faced the joint problem of the disposal of time and the necessity to produce some kind of structure into their lives where little such structure was externally imposed. And thirdly, more generally, they were faced with the problem of understanding a range of questions related to their position. Why were they unemployed? Why were many of the people living around them and the same age as them unemployed? What was special about the West End? In other words they had to come to terms with who they were and what their relationship to the wider society was. And it is possible to see much of their daily routine, their 'views', their behaviour, and their style in the context of these problems and questions.

HANGING ABOUT

Because of the position in which they found themselves the boys spent much of their time hanging about in or around Luke Street. 'Hanging about' has often been described in the literature on working-class male adolescence, although the boredom and ennui of it has been over-stressed. For instance James Patrick in his Glasgow study shows that 'jis dossin' was the main activity of the gang he observed.[6] And Phil Cohen argues:

> Hanging about, doing nothing is something totally incomprehensible to many people and a clear sign that there is something wrong . . . But what appears to outsiders to be just mucking about to kids themselves is a natural and not unenjoyable way of spending time. At least not as boring as school or work; in fact the kind of interactions that go in these situations are more creative than is often supposed.[7]

Although there were individual differences the daily routine of the boys on the corner followed a fairly set pattern. Except on 'signing on morning' or when one of them had to be in court, most of the boys got up fairly late and there was rarely any activity on the corner or in Luke Street before 12.00 or 12.30. At one stage, it was Brown's practice to go down to Eddy's house and wake him up at one o'clock. During the dinner hour some of the boys would arrive at Casey's and either hang about on the corner or if they had the money drink half a pint of lager at the bar. By about 12.30, there would be quite a few of the boys about and most of them would know what the others were doing. From then onwards the day might follow the typical pattern of:

2.30 – 4.00	A bus ride down town and walking around the centre of town. Possibly a cup of tea in the large working-men's cafe in the centre of town.
4.00 – 5.00	Back to Luke Street and hanging about outside one of the boy's houses. Watching people coming back from work. Luke Street was active at this time of day, and it was a time for catching up on what had happened. It was a time for finding out whether anyone had found work or whether there were any jobs going anywhere.
5.00 – 7.00	Back home for tea.
6.30	Back on to the corner. Hanging about Luke Street. Possibly into Casey's for a glass of lager. By 9 o'clock Casey's and the corner were typically crowded and this would continue until closing time. After closing time, some of the older men would join the boys and stand about on the corner. By about 11.30 the corner would be empty and there would probably be just a few of the boys left there. After a visit to the late-night chip shop up the road, the boys would either go home or several of them might stay 'walking the streets' until one or two in the morning.

Apart from this everyday routine, there was the dole to be picked up. The following abstract from my fieldnotes describes one such 'dole morning':

We spent quite a long time waiting in the dole this morning. Lombo was there as was his elder brother and father. It was the first time that Lombo had received his money at the men's dole and everybody was giving him advice on the different forms he would have to fill in. Eddy told me jokingly that 'us older ones have got to look after the young ones'.

In contrast to the hours of hanging about and yet the

product of the same circumstances were the occasions on which the boys in their own words 'went wild' and broke out from the contraints that their position imposed on them. The following is a description of a night out with the boys in the middle of August:

The corner was crowded tonight. There were perhaps as many as fifteen of the boys there at one one time. Everybody was in good spirits and at about half-past nine Frankie suggested that some of us might stay up the night and go for a swim in the docks. At about 11.30 the older men had left the corner. There were six of us left there – Kenny, Eddy, Brown, Frankie, Frannie and me. We went up into Cambridge Road and sat outside Brown's house for a little while. Then Frankie went back to Luke Street saying he was going to get his I.R.A. beret.[8] He came back to us and we all returned to Luke Street. Frankie and the rest seemed to go into top gear and we started running up and down Luke Street singing 'King Finian's army is deaded, King Finian's army is deaded'. Frankie changed the words to 'Luke Street's army is deaded, Luke Street's army is deaded'. Frankie was leading the dancing. By this time one or two people were leaning out of their upstairs windows in the street. As we ran down the street Frankie was shouting 'Who's coming swimming, who's coming swimming'. Mrs —, who was leaning out of her bedroom window, shouted 'No, I'm not coming swimming with you – we're going to swim in bed.' We crossed the Dock Road and keeping close into the wall to avoid being seen by the dock guards, went down to the waterside. To get into the closed part of the dock, we had to lean out and swing around the spikes. We then went along the water side to the empty dock which the boys always swim in. We stripped off when we got there and spent half an hour diving in and out of the polluted water. One of the attractions of this dock is that it has a pulley on which it is possible to swing out on to the open water and then dive. The night's activities ended about 2.30.

During my time with the boys there were other examples

of going 'wild'. On one occasion, Brown talked about the previous night's activities: 'We were out again last night. Really late. We were up on — hill. Going wild. We were all running through this graveyard. Masso was screeching and jumping out at everybody. We didn't get down here until 3 o'clock. We'd do anything for a laugh.' And for a few weeks during the summer it was common for one of the boys to go over into the docks and 'see what's come in today'. On several occasions, vehicles were taken out of the docks and driven across to Luke Street. Here Jacko describes to me what had happened the night before in Luke Street.

> You should have been down last night. Danny drove this wagon over from the docks. We were all going up and down the street. Danny was driving. I was on the back. Hanging on. Everybody else was on the top. Everybody was leaning out of their windows shouting. We were going to make the lorry into the barricade for the 'no go' area but Danny said no. Frankie tried to persuade him but he said no.

The main characteristic of the boys' lives was therefore, hanging about – an activity which was not unpleasant in itself and to which they brought their own particular style and humour. And the very routine of where to hang about, when to hang about and who to hang about with introduced some kind of structure into their lives. Hanging about was also an active business to the extent that the boys moved from one location to another and within the narrow confines allowed them could find 'things to do'. But although the routine was occasionally interspersed with more active sessions their basic position was one of being on the street with no money and nowhere to go.

THE TRADITION OF 'WILDNESS'

The analysis of even small-scale cultural traditions presents problems. What are the components of the tradition? Where does it come from? How is it handed down? Why is one individual or group affected by it and not another? Such questions do not lend themselves easily to precise answers. Also, this study was conducted at a particular point in time and the development of certain traditions had to be inferred primarily from present-day 'views'. This is, of course, part of the wider problem of a study which attempts to put an historical perspective on the changing relationship between contexts and meanings.

But to understand the position of the boys who hung about regularly on the corner it is necessary to see them as part of the historical development of Luke Street. The boys understood that they were the inheritors of the activities and the way of life of previous groups of their age in the neighbourhood. In their own words they were 'carrying it on' and men in their twenties supported this recognition by admitting that they had 'been wild like the rest of them'. In the slightly different terminology of a local youth leader, 'there's always a new group to take over what I call the cabbage patch. One group grows up and another takes its place.'

Like other people in the neighbourhood the boys on the corner were in fact able to pinpoint reasonably accurately the date when their predecessors in the area had begun to 'go wild' and the West End had become increasingly the focus of incidents with the police. Some were able to do this from the direct experience of having been moved into the area as young children and having grown up in it and others from the past reputations of individuals and groups. Although one or two of the boys asserted that 'it's always been wild down our way – always', others had a consistent picture of it beginning to get 'bad' eight or nine years previously, in the mid-1960s and getting increasingly worse until the late 1960s. The date of the origin of this 'tradition' is, therefore, consistent with the development and change of the neighbourhood in the late 1950s and 1960s as indicated in Chapter 2. Here for instance Mal, whose family arrived in Luke Street in 1965 describes the development of the 'tradition' in a taped conversation:

O.G. You must have been about ten when you came down there. What can you remember?

Mal   When we first moved up there – quiet. But a year after we lived up there all hell broke loose until about what, four years ago.

O.G.   When you say all hell broke loose, what do you mean?

Mal   Lots of mini riots . . . it was getting so bad everybody was afraid to go out at night.

This process was seen to have reached its culmination in the late 1960s and the local boys looked back on this as something of a golden age when everything was happening. In part, this was associated with the widespread adoption in Crossley, or elsewhere, of the skinhead style. The boys who I knew had regarded themselves, in conversation at least, as the younger members of the general group known as the West End Book Boys (the 'W.E.B.B.') and by 1971–2, were regarding themselves as the 'last ones' because 'everybody else has been put inside or left'.

And although some of the boys on the corner were approaching twenty they were in the words of one of them 'staying wild'. The boys looked back with a degree of nostalgia to the 'good old days when we were all skinheads'. And there were a number of stories associated with this era. Here one of the boys explains one of the routines:

> We used to wait behind the buses at the other end of Luke Street. And when any cunt come up we'd jump out at them. We'd say have you got a cigarette mate? And they'd say no. Have you got a match mate? And they'd say no. And then we'd say well you'd better have this then and smash them right in the face.

Another described a more original form of this activity:

> What we'd do. Everybody would get behind the bushes and one of us would put on an old coat and an old hat. Then he'd hobble along the road and when he passed the bushes everybody would jump out at him and pretend to boot him. What would happen then is somebody driving along would stop and come to the rescue. Then the one

who was wearing the coat would throw it off and everybody
would turn on the bloke who had stopped.

For the boys, therefore, the neighbourhood was associated
with a tradition of adolescent lawlessness. The strength of
this association was nicely illustrated one night when I was
with Eddy and Brown. Kenny came and joined us and started
to pretend to beat us up. As he gave us a mock booting
he shouted: 'I was a good boy till I came down the West
End. I used to be an angel when I lived in — Street. But
now I'm down here I go wild, wild, wild. It's this place
that's done it. I'm wild, wild.' He continued to pretend to
lay into us. Eddy looked on amusedly.

The boys on the corner believed themselves to be the inheritors of a tradition which appeared to have its origin ten
years previously in the particular circumstances of all their
families being 'put up the West End'. And since that date
several successive groups had gone through the 'wild' period
of late adolescence.

There is one other point in relation to this tradition of
wildness which I consider very important. It was a *public*
tradition – something that was only activated in a public
setting. It is possible to distinguish between two broad types
of social world that the boys operated in and this distinction
offers insights not only for the way in which their everyday
lives were structured but also for the way in which they
came into contact with authority. First there were those
situations in which the boys were simply 'passing the time'
or 'getting by' with members of their own families or other
people from their neighbourhood. Secondly there were those
public situations in which the boys were in contact with the
representatives of authority from outside the neighbourhood.
And it was these times that were particularly problematic
for them and in which they developed their self-conception
of being 'outside the law'. Therefore to talk about the boys
being 'anti-authority' confuses more than it helps. There were
well-articulated authority patterns actually within Luke
Street and the boys were responsive to them. Thus for instance
the person whom the outside world characterises in a
unidimensional fashion as the vandal, football hooligan

or skinhead tends in Casey's to leave aside these identities. In fact one of the things that struck me during my time in Luke Street was that in the privacy of their own world the boys could laugh at the identities the outside world gave them and could stand back from the cultural tradition of 'wildness'.

SUMMARY

It is necessary to see the 'hanging about', the occasional 'wildness' and the cultural imperative of 'hardness' in its structural context. They did not develop in a vacuum, nor should the humour that the boys developed about their position be simply taken at its face value. That would be to support the external stereotype of the boys and the area as one which was in a basic sense 'abnormal'. The boys' reactions should be seen in the context of the realities of life for young unemployed people in the West End. Life in Luke Street was hard but as in any situation from which there is no immediate exit the boys tried to come to terms with their position and salvage something from it in terms of their own personal identity. And one of the most realistic ways to do this was to 'see the funny side of things' and make a virtue out of necessity. Elliot Liebow talking about life on 'Tally's Corner' in Washington D.C. has accurately captured this reversal of perspective and the making of virtue out of necessity. 'Here where the measure of a man is considerably smaller and where weaknesses are somehow turned upside down and almost magically transformed into strengths, he can, once again be a man among men.'[9]

The purpose of this chapter has been to introduce the boys on Casey's corner, and see them as one group in a long line of such groups. It has also been to indicate some of the facts about the position in which they found themselves and the cultural contexts in which they operated. The reason for doing this has not been to describe in general detail their everyday lives. Such an exercise would be 'interesting', but if honestly conducted would produce much that was unexceptional. Rather the purpose of the chapter has been to suggest some of the characteristics of the boys' lives essential for an analysis of their occasional problematic contact with authority. On the basis of my observations four such characteristics can be suggested: (i) The boys inherited a tradition that adolescence in Luke Street was a 'wild period'. Others before them had 'gone through it'. This tradition would appear to date from the early 1960s and be linked with the circumstances surrounding the construction and decline of Luke Street. (ii) This tradition was also linked with the far more general male culture of which the boys were a part. This culture evaluated the 'hard man' positively and upheld a degree of scepticism about authority and the way it operated. (iii) The effects of these traditions were accentuated by the boys' unemployment. They were in a position in which the only way of spending time was to 'hang about' on the Street. (iv) Casey's corner offered them a focal point.

7

THE STRUCTURE OF DELINQUENT INCIDENTS

When you see a gang of youths in that area it usually means trouble.

> Local police constable giving evidence in court

The coppers come around here looking for trouble: it's simple, less coppers, less trouble.

> Mal

When specific incidents are described in the sociological literature on either adolescence delinquency or community life in general it is usually for illustrative rather than analytical purposes. Incidents are taken to indicate the *general* nature of a situation rather than analysed as important elements of ongoing life which develop from and change individual's perceptions of their social world and thus produce the potential for further similar events.[1] But to obtain an accurate idea of the logic and process of what the wider society categorises as delinquent it is essential to acknowledge the fluidity of different local contexts and to give accounts of different events and the way in which they are inter-related. And an obvious accompaniment to the examination of this occasional delinquent behaviour in its actual setting is to see it through the eyes of the participants themselves. Because boys such as those in Luke Street come at the bottom of three credibility piles – they are lower class, they are young and they are 'offenders' – their action is given little credit for having an internal logic and consistency. Also the analysis of specific incidents is valuable at two distinct levels. First, it is important to analyse circumstances which produce the coming together of conflicting groups or individuals and the way in which such confrontations develop and terminate. Secondly, it is important to analyse the way in which such incidents become part of local consciousness, and thus mould or crystallise perceptions of situations and in turn increase the possibility of further problematic contact.

The examination of these various processes and the way in which they can culminate in the incident allows delinquent activity to be seen in its structural context than in terms of preconceived general criteria. By abstracting adolescence out of their life – contexts and categorising them as delinquent many studies have discounted the circumstances of individual neighbourhoods. Indeed sociologists who have categorised groups of young people as either 'delinquent' or 'non-delinquent' have done violence to the reality of the lives led by their subjects. In particular they have failed to recognise the 'normality' of the majority of their subjects' behaviour. For instance in terms of a sample of adolescent behaviour in the West End of Crossley the occasional incidents between the police and the local boys were completely untypical. The examination of behaviour defined as delinquent also counteracts the exaggerated importance attributed to 'attitudes' in delinquency research. The implicit assumption of such research is that there must be something consistently abnormal about the way a person looks at the world for him to be involved in delinquent activity and his 'attitudes' have seemed the best way to understand this consistent abnormality.

My intention is therefore to look at the context in which delinquency occurs, the structural origins of that context and its subjective meanings. In doing this my perspective is in line with the suggestions made by Cohen for the extensions necessary to traditional subcultural explanations of adolescent group violence and vandalism. Three of these extensions were seen by Cohen to be (i) 'certain situations and contexts become defined in such a way that violent responses are tolerated, expected, or even called for. This observation is commonplace; the point is that such definitions of others operate as causal factors, or at least contingencies, at crucial stages of the juvenile's involvement in violence or vandalism.'[2] (ii) 'Much juvenile group violence is highly localised and an understanding of its generation must take into account specific ecological and historical traditions.'[3] (iii) 'Related to both these first two points is the need to understand the very different contexts in which juvenile violence might occur. In both popular and academic explanations one sometimes finds a type of reductionism which might be called the "pool of deviants assumption"; the same sort of youths are going around committing the whole range of property damage and personal violence . . . such an analysis implies that the context of the behaviour is fortuitous.'[4]

The boys on Casey's corner hung about on the street and occasionally got into 'trouble' with the police. This and the next chapter examine the nature of this 'trouble'. Typically the boys were involved in delinquent acts which can be described as non-material. They did not appear in court on charges of theft but on more nebulous and sub-jectively assessed charges such as causing a disturbance, assault or resisting arrest. Thus although some of them occasionally 'made a few bob' on stolen property the main reason for their court appearances was incidents on the street. And typically these incidents involved direct confrontation with the police. My argument is that the boys were likely to come into contact with the police on the street because of their unstructured and public lives. I would also argue that the representatives of external authority were particularly sensitive about their behaviour on the street. The result of these two factors were the incidents that took place and these incidents had severe effects on the lives of the boys and also increased the external stereotype of the existence of a 'bad' area. The boys were not so much the victims of a formal labelling process but were subject to a less distinct form of labelling on the streets.

The examination of incidents on the street offers a perspective which can combine an analysis of the character-istics of the situations and the specific orientations of the individuals involved in it. It thus allows a move away from a static analysis of what are thought to be the consistent 'attitudes' of 'delinquents'. Such incidents in Luke Street occurred infrequently and against a blackcloth of normal day-to-day life in the neighbourhood. The boys could typically hang about in the neighbourhood for long periods and then in certain circumstances an incident could develop quickly and just as quickly terminate. An incident that could take less than a minute to be enacted could have severe consequences for those involved and could play a part in structuring future conceptions of the position in which the boys found themselves. David Matza has accurately pin-pointed the importance of such incidents in this latter respect: 'His knowledge of local history supplies him with an initial set of incidents on which he may subsequently build a memory file that collects injustices.'[5]

The following chapter is based on my observation of incidents in the Luke Street neighbourhood[6] and also on taped conversations with the boys who participated in them.[7] Although members of the police were not interviewed formerly in relation to specific incidents I was involved in a number of discussions with police officers in respect of their policy towards the neighbourhood and witnessed the court cases where the police offered their version of 'reality' in relation to the incidents described. Also and most crucially I was in a position to witness their activity on the street.

In using taped conversations with the boys to describe these incidents I am aware of the problem that in spite of easy relations the boys might have misrepresented the 'facts' to me. But this is a difficulty of all forms of research which relies on words and unlike most other researchers I was in the position to substantiate what was said by further conversations and observations. And in fact the boys' *subjective* interpretations of the incidents they were involved in are analytically more useful than an objective assessment of the various 'moves' in each incident, even if such an objective assessment was possible. Indeed an incident of police–adolescent contact on the street is a striking example of a situation in which everybody must produce their own version of reality. And in fact I believe that the interpretations of the incidents offered to me by the boys were similar to those that were employed in their everyday lives and amongst themselves. I support this claim by their consistency over time and between individuals. The nature of the 'accounts' of these incidents must also be seen as of importance in that they give insights into the beliefs and internal cohesion of the group. C. Wright Mills long ago stressed the role of such accounts in maintaining group expectations and operating as a motivating force for further action.[8]

OCCASIONAL INCIDENTS

Life in Luke Street progressed without major incident for long periods and then a combination of circumstances led to a confrontation between the police and a boy or groups of boys. And the incidents in which the boys were involved stood out very clearly in their minds against the backcloth of their everyday routine of 'hanging about' and provided the basis of the 'talk' that was a central ingredient of that everyday routine.

Although in a time perspective their contact with the police was sporadic and short-lived the perceived characteristics of this contact remained with them constantly. Incidents or words that to the outsider would seem insignificant were invested with importance and each fresh incident was interpreted within the framework of the boys' belief that the police were 'out to get us', that they were 'interfering where they had no business', or that their methods were corrupt. The arrival of a police officer or a police car in the neighbourhood created immediate interest on the part of the boys. This interest was probably at its most extreme when a member of the police came into Casey's itself, either following up a specific incident or hoping to obtain general information. Not only were they recognised as such but they were the focus of suspicious attention. For instance, one evening at about seven o'clock I was sitting in Casey's with one of the boys. He pointed out that a plain clothes policeman was at the bar. Several minutes later another one came in and ordered a drink but did not speak to his companion. Through the looks and glances that were circulating everybody knew they were police.

Occasionally the interest that the police aroused could

lead to direct contact with the boys. The following three sections of taped conversations describe contact of this nature which was a direct consequence of the boys 'hanging about':

Frankie   We were walking home about three o'clock in the morning and there waš about six of us. We'd been down to that chippie that's open to four o'clock to get ciggies. This panda came up behind us doing about four miles an hour just following about six yards behind. Trying to be funny. It followed us the whole way up. Just following us. We cut across the field trying to lose them because they were being funny with us. Then we got down to Hughie's house. We were inside the gate and they were just sitting in the car there looking at us trying to be funny. Hughie brought us out seven cups of tea into the garden and we sat there drinking it. Then they started to be funny with us and got out their flasks of tea. After half-an-hour the panda went off round the block and came back again and they put their fingers up [i.e. V-sign].

Eddy   We were standing on the corner the other night and this Bedford van came round. It stopped right by us and me and Brown thought they were dockers going to ask the way. Any rate this bloke gets out and says what are you doing there. I said, I'm only standing here, pal. He says don't fucking call me pal. Then he said 'fuck off home – I'm the police.' They're coming round in all sorts now.

Brown   Last week I was sitting on the wall with Kenny. A panda comes along and says what are you two doing there. So we said we're waiting for a bus. So he says if a fucking bus stops there I'll give you a pound. Now piss off.

Occasionally this kind of contact could be transformed into direct hostility and this could escalate into one of the boys being taken in. Here Eddy describes such a sequence:

we were on the corner . . . and we saw this jam-buttie[9] car. So I shouted fuck off coppers, go home. So it drives back and the copper says 'Who's the big mouth?' So I said what you on about. So he said who's the big mouth who shouted fuck off copper at me. So I said it wasn't me. So he said get off home. So I said I'm just going up the road for some chips. Then I said O.K. we're just going home. So I turned round to go to the Dock Road and he says you live in Cambridge Road. So I said no I don't. And he grabs hold of my shirt and says go home or I'll have you. So I start walking down to the Dock Road and then he grabs hold of me and puts me in the car. Next morning I'm up for disorderly behaviour.

The boys believed that if the police wanted to take anybody in it was easy for them to do so:

Jacko You've got no chance against the coppers. Like Saturday night at about two in the morning we were coming back from — and they push you just so you'll say 'fuck off' and they can drag you in then ... They only cause trouble when they come down here. The bobbies will go for any bastard around here. If you say you come from the West End they say 'Oh that'll do us.'

Eddy You get no peace with the coppers. There was Danny, Brown and me on the corner. Next minute a jeep comes up. He says 'get off the corner'. We said we aren't doing nothing. He said get off the corner. They just wanted to argue so they could pull us in. They wanted to get their own back. There's no enjoyment. You're going for a night out and you're walking down the street and they're stopping and saying where have you fucking been.

The way in which the police were believed to 'pick on' the West End and Luke Street in particular was central to the way the boys perceived incidents such as these. The boys believed that the police had a continual 'down' on them and that they treated a person from the Luke Street neighbourhood differently than a person from another area. Because of the police's increased surveillance of the neighbourhood and their different 'attitude' to people who lived there the boys believed that two identical people could act in identical ways but that the one from Luke Street would find himself in contact with the law. Here Frankie and Eddy describe the way in which they believed the police 'victimised' the West End:

Eddy   You get fuck all around our end. There's no peace around here for the lads. You can't walk nowhere, there's bobbies coming at you – where d'you come from? West End. Right get in the car they say. Then they take you down the Bridewell and charge you for disorderly behaviour or disturbing the peace. They'll get something on you . . . It's going to come now so that we can't walk the streets unless we get picked up. Lads up in — [one of the new estates] never get that trouble. Me and Brown was down town one night and they were just passing us. We saw one panda and he did nothing. Then half-an-hour later we saw the same panda when we were in the West End and he stopped and said what're you doing around here . . . they've called us West End twats, West End misfits . . . All it is is victimisation of the West End.

Frankie   What's in the paper every weekend. It's only the West End. You never hear of — or — like last Saturday, walking back from the centre of town. The nearer we got to the West End the more pandas pulled up.

Eddy   Police never pick up other lads. It's always the West End. No wonder when they come around there's always bottles flying at them.

Although the boys recognised individual policemen and could have strong feelings about them because of previous incidents, the resentment against the police was generalised. A member of the police was automatically regarded with suspicion and hostility. The best way to illustrate this is by the position of a policeman known locally as Big Jim whom the boys regarded as a hostile intruder. He was regarded, publicly at least, as personifying the scheming nature of the police. For instance, the story was told of how Big Jim had gone to a boy who claimed he had been hit across the nose by a policeman and asked whether we was able to remember his number, knowing the boy had no chance of doing so. Both his local fame and the attitude towards him on the part of the boys were nicely illustrated by the chalked sign which appeared on the pavement of Luke Street one day – ALL BIG JIMS ARE BASTARDS. And here Jacko describes his attitude to Big Jim:

> Jim thinks we're like that [crossing his fingers] . . . But he's a fucking nut case. He starts to get friendly with the lads. He says what you drinking and all that. He gives them a few bob and then he says 'Oh by the way I've heard Casey's got done the other night.' Then he says 'don't know anything about it, do you?'

The incidents that the boys describe here were typical of the kind of short-lived contact that they had with the police. If a group of boys were on the street and they were approached by the police there was the likelihood of an incident. And although that incident could last perhaps only a matter of seconds it could have severe repercussions on the lives of the individuals concerned. Some of the above descriptions show how an incident could lead to a charge of disorderly behaviour and is it in this context that the boys' extreme sensitivity about these contacts becomes intelligible. Their sensitivity about gestures, looks and words is understandable in that it was these kind of contacts, if either side allowed them to develop, that brought the boys to court.

The boys recognised the nature of their contact with the police and realised what kinds of situation could produce conflict and how that conflict could develop. For instance, here Rappo describes a chance meeting in the street: 'This sergeant comes up to me and says hello Rappo. I didn't say a thing, not a thing. I just kept on walking. One thing can lead to another – you know what I mean. Before we knew where we were we'd be having a go.' But the boys also believed that if a member of the police 'started' then they were also entitled to 'have a go':

Eddy I wouldn't let no copper hit me, unless I hit them back.

Lombo   I was walking down the street and I didn't know the copper was after me. The copper asked me where I was going. They asked if I had anything on me. I said why, do you want to search me. They said are you trying to be funny. So I smashed him right in the face and tried to leg it.

The 'naturalness' of this reaction was also indicated by one of the boys' older brothers: 'Say if there's a group of fifty kids, you know lads hanging around and a couple of coppers come in to break them up: well it's dead certain that one of these lads will have a go at him, take a swing at him. It's natural.'

Contact with the police on the street had the potential therefore of quickly developing into an incident and these incidents could lead to one or more of the boys being taken in. In these situations the boys clearly regarded themselves as being involved in a conflict in which there were two 'sides', the interests of one being directly opposed to the interests of the other. On the one side were the police, representatives of external authority and on the other were the boys. The boys believed they were 'in the right' and they were 'getting their own back' on the police. And in this the boys' belief that they were unfairly discriminated against by the police because of their area takes on significance. To the boys it was always someone else who 'started it' and if arrested 'they wouldn't mind if they'd done anything'. And related to this was the boys' perception that they were united in their endeavours in as much as it was a matter of chance whether or not an individual was apprehended because 'the police just get any cunt they can lay their hands on'. This is the key to the boys' subjective experience of the incident. Their reactions were considered to be a justified response to the perceived attributes of the police and in this sense any feeling of the 'wrongness' of their action was neutralised.

TEN DAYS IN APRIL

Not all the incidents in Luke Street were isolated events. In fact it is a characteristic of these incidents, because of the tensions that they produce, that they tend to cluster.[10]

Occasionally, there could be a series of incidents of police–
boy contact over a number of days resulting from a build-up
in police activity. Such build-ups and corresponding declines
in police activity were a characteristic of life in Luke Street.
A senior officer quoted in the *Crossley News* described such
build-ups in the following way: 'Whenever trouble occurs –
and vandalism occurs in varying parts of the borough day
by day, we endeavour to put more policemen on that beat
and increase patrols.' This section looks therefore at a series
of incidents which took place in the neighbourhood over
a period of ten days and were very much linked to such
a build-up in police activity. All of the incidents described
took place on or very near Casey's corner.

During the ten days there was a major build-up of police
activity in the neighbourhood and as a result of this a
sequence of confrontations between the Luke Street boys and
the police occurred. The sequence of events that led to the
final confrontation was the result of an incident which is itself
of interest as an illustration both of some of the difficulties
of the area and the way that the press dealt with it. Several
weeks previously the police found three boys in one of the
unoccupied houses in the Dock Road. The house next to
it was occupied by a widow, a Mrs S. She was one of the
few people in the neighbourhood with a telephone and it
was believed that she rang the police and told them that
the house was being 'vandalised'. In the following days
there were intermittent cases of small groups of younger
boys throwing stones at her house. This failed to attract much
interest in the neighbourhood until a lengthy description
of it appeared in the *Crossley News*:

HOOLIGANS IN WAR OF TERROR ON WIDOW

A war of terror is being waged against a lonely 70 year
old woman by a gang of teenage hooligans because they
think she informed on young vandals. The terrified woman
Mrs S. of Dock Road, Crossley, said 'I know who is doing
this but I am frightened to say anything.'

The actual incidents and more particularly the publicity

given to them led to a rapid build-up of police activity in the Luke Street neighbourhood, beginning on the weekend and most noticeable in the immediate vicinity of Luke Street. The clearest indication was the frequency of police patrols in the neighbourhood. The cars would typically cut the corner and drive through Luke Street rather than taking the more obvious route along the Dock Road. This as usual caused interest and there was a general feeling that something was 'on'. When a car passed Casey's people drinking there would come out and stand on the corner to follow its movements. The build-up in police activity was particularly resented because it was believed that outsiders were involved in 'vandalising' the house and that the younger boys involved in the 'campaign of terror' were not from Luke Street. As a result of the increase in police activity there were a number of individual incidents over the first weekend.

I was directly involved in the next confrontation which occurred on the Monday night at about 10 o'clock. I had come out of Casey's and was standing out on the corner with six of the boys. We were standing just off the pavement in the Dock Road and talking and 'seeing what was happening'. There had been a lot of police patrols earlier in the evening and after some minutes a panda car drove up the Dock Road and parked about twenty yards from us. We carried on talking and after stopping for about three minutes the car drove very slowly through our group, forcing us back onto the pavement, after which it stopped and one of the constables got out of the car and told us we were 'loitering'. We told him we were 'doing nothing – just talking'. He replied that if we wanted to talk we would have to 'walk up and down the street'. An argument developed and some of the men came out of Casey's and stood at the door listening. After arguing for about three minutes the constable finally got back into his car and started to drive off. As he did one of the boys gave the nearside back wing of the car a kick. The car stopped immediately and the constable jumped out and said 'right that's it'. More people had by this time appeared at Casey's door. The police asked us who did it and no one answered. After another several minutes of questioning the police took names and addresses and then drove off.

Police activity continued in the area and the frequent patrols became a major talking point over the following days. The most significant aspect of the 'talk' was that the boys believed that the main reason for the increased patrols was that the police were determined to 'clear up the rest of the West End' and 'put inside' the remaining Luke Street boys. As Eddy said at the time: 'They're just waiting to get us. We're the last few really. They've got everybody else and put them inside. Now they're just waiting to get something on us.' In the middle of the week the police appeared to adopt a new approach and 'plain clothes' policemen started to patrol the area. This was readily recognised by the boys:

Eddy The night [Wednesday] when me and Brown were coming down there was two in the street. We crossed over and asked them what you knocking around the West End in plain clothes for now? They told us to mind our own business and get on our way.

Frankie They're following you around now. The bobbies around here look as though they've been stabbed.

And perhaps the best indication of this resentment of plain clothes policemen was the appearance by the end of the week on the wall of Casey's the slogan: FUCK OFF PLAIN CLOTHES COPPERS – WE AIN'T SOFT.[11]

By Wednesday evening the resentment had developed further and there was a feeling that 'something big is going to happen'. On that evening Frankie was involved in an incident with two plain clothes policemen in which they claimed that he was going to throw a bottle at them. Frankie described how the incident developed in the following way: 'He grabbed me by the wrist and I said get off you're fucking breaking my wrist. He said that's another charge, disorderly behaviour . . . You may as well say you're guilty before you go to court if you come from around here.' Much later the same night there was a further incident:

Eddy Wednesday night about half-one I was standing in our front [i.e. small front garden to house] waiting for —

to come in. I was inside my own front garden. They [the police] said fucking get away. I said this is my own house . . . I had the key to get in and I showed it to them. Well if you can't stand outside your own door . . .

Frankie You're fucking scared to walk the streets with these bobbies around here. I am anyway. You're scared to walk out 'cause you'll get picked up for loitering. You should be able to walk around at night like. We usually only stay outside our houses and they come . . . There were about eight pandas around here last Wednesday when I came home. There were pandas, jeeps and dog cars.

There was a further potential incident the same night. The mother of one of the boys told me: 'That week when all the trouble was on a copper pulled up by our Hughie. He was sitting by the steps and he said what do you want. The copper said straight away do you want to make something of it because if you do I can get twenty witnesses here in half a minute.'

These then were a series of 'incidents' that occurred within the space of less than a week in the Luke Street neighbourhood. Their occurrence and more generally the level of police activity in the neighbourhood were a major talking point and there was a high degree of resentment. The boys and many of the adults in the area believed that the police were operating in an unjustifiable manner. The boys not only believed that the frequency of the police patrols was far too high but also that the patrols had specific orders to 'clean up the area'. They believed that the police were 'pushing them' so that they in turn would retaliate and could then be 'put away'. They thus anticipated the way things would go and indicated their belief in the logical outcome of events. As Frankie said: 'One of them's gonna get run in. One of them's gonna go. There's gonna be some fucker's going to work a knife into one of them.'

The final confrontation when it occurred was not quite so dramatic as Frankie anticipated. I had been in Casey's on Thursday evening and left the corner at just before 11 o'clock. Tasker had also been drinking in Casey's. By about

11.30 the group had apparently reformed and there were about ten to fifteen boys and other locals 'talking football' on the corner. At about 11.45 two plain clothes policemen came past on one of their now familiar patrols. They stopped and started talking and the conversation remained at a reasonably friendly level. Eddy tells the story from when Tasker joined the group:

> There were two bobbies walking down the street . . . we were all on the corner talking about football and . . . all that. And the bobbies started talking to us. Jimmy brings up the idea of having a match between Casey's and the police. It was going on alright. Then Tasker comes along and it was going alright. Tasker was talking to Jimmy about football and said joking like you can't play football and Jimmy said you can't play football. Then the police join in and it's getting nasty. So the policeman radios 'Panda to Casey's' and says I'm taking you in. And Tasker says I'm not talking to you. And the bobby had a go at Tasker and Tasker has a swipe at him and they end up on the floor.[12] Well anyone would do that wouldn't they if a bobby had a swipe at them. Well the other pandas arrived. Then we saw the panda car window shatter. Anybody could have done it. Everybody was watching from the gardens and windows in the Dock Road and they're full of bricks those gardens. All the time Tasker is fighting with the bobby on the floor and some of the lads are trying to get him off. Tasker's Mum comes out and tries to stop it, but they took Tasker off in the panda.

After Thursday night there were no more incidents with the police. Not only did the police patrols become less frequent but also because of the possible seriousness of the policeman's injuries and the impending court cases the principal participants were reluctant to become involved in further confrontations. But there was a general feeling that the police 'got what they deserved'. As Frankie said on Friday, 'They look for trouble and they got it last night.'

This series of incidents culminating in the policeman's injury led to a crystallisation and development of the beliefs that the local boys had of the police. The police were not only thought to be 'victimising the West End' but also to be using unscrupulous methods to do so. Added to this there were a number of specific beliefs about the incidents. One of the most prevalent of these that developed in the following days was that the policeman had not really been hurt. Also there was a strong belief that not only had the police been attempting to 'get' the small group of remaining Luke Street boys, but also that members of certain families had been victimised because they had a 'famous name'. Without realising it, Frankie summed up the local feelings that the police had made a bad situation worse when he said a few days later: 'Everybody's unemployed around here. Now they're putting them all inside.'

As a result of the Thursday night confrontation two of the boys were sent to Borstal and another was sent to prison for nine months. It was two months before the court cases were finally completed and the events of the Thursday evening, therefore, remained part of the 'consciousness' of the neighbourhood for that period. Frankie was also found guilty on a charge of throwing a bottle at the policemen and fined.

SOME ENTERTAINMENT IN LUKE STREET

The previous pages have described incidents which were similar in that they involved hostile police–boy contact on the street. By way of contrast this section describes an incident which started as a family affair and was perceived as a case of the police 'interfering where they had no business'. The incident took place in the middle of a summer afternoon in Luke Street and resulted from a family argument. It is described here in a taped conversation with Mal, the principal participant.

Mal I'd come back. I'd been out since three in the morning and come back at three in the afternoon. I'd come back and our Johnny was on the roof with his mate Frank. Anyway I had to go up to fix the aerial.
O.G. To fix the . . .?

Mal The aerial. I said as I had to fix the aerial I said I'll go up now instead of later on. I told the two of them to come down. His mate did. But Johnny was still there. So I went to shift him. Any rate he hit me with a chain. A bicycle chain that is. If I'd got him I would have thrown him off that roof, that's a dead cert. We were chasing him round the chimney pots and that sort of thing and he started throwing bricks at me. I'm not usually violent. But I picked up these two chimney pots and I threw them at him. And they are big chimney pots. Then our Jeannie [his sister] came out. And by that time a crowd of fifty had gathered.

O.G. In the street?

Mal In the street. And by the time the panda came there was 150.

O.G. Who called the panda?

Mal You know little Roberts? The smallest one. It was him. Cheeky little git. Any rate a copper came up and told me to get down. By this time our Johnny had sneaked down and by this time I didn't feel like getting down. I was really mad. So I said 'Go to hell.' I knew by his reputation what a bastard he was. A few minutes later another panda came. That had three in it. Then another came and that had four in it; so that makes eight coppers altogether ... Well now the coppers get in the back garden, they barged right through the door without a Tom, Dick or Harry or anything. Any rate this copper was in the back and another followed him and another. The crowd was also in the back; now the entry was packed out. You know entertainment.[13] Any rate they called up the fire engine.

O.G. The panda called it up?

Mal There was this particular copper who tried to get up on the fire ladder to get me. Well for a bit I held him off ... in the end he got down so I retired to the top of the roof for a sit down. Any rate he got up again. I was stupid there because I could have got down then. Any rate I was going to get down on the pipe. But this copper climbs up the pipe and gets hold of my leg ... so I got down after that. Anyway no sooner had I got down and they were pushing me through the house ...

O.G. The crowd were still there?

Mal Aye. The crowd were still there. Any rate seeing me get kicked in the face they got you know a bit mad. They had to keep the lads back, the lads were edging for a bit of a smack-up with the coppers.

The other lads were in fact joining in by this time. As one of the Luke Street women who witnessed the incident told me: 'They played the game of nicking the keys from the police car and handing them round till they arrived back on the bonnet of the car. . . and then a copper got his helmet knocked off . . . you can say what you want but whenever the police come down our street there's always some fun.'

While this was happening Mal was taken to the police station and charged with assault and soon afterwards the police left the street. The whole incident had taken place in a matter of minutes and life returned to normal in Luke Street. But there was yet one more 'story' of a confrontation between the 'local lads' and the police. And one more Luke Street boy was in court. Mal was fined £35 for this incident.

AUTHORITY, IDENTITY AND ACTION

The incidents described in this chapter are relatively minor and certainly do not correspond to the picture presented of such delinquent events in the media. And yet it is just these kinds of events which lead individuals into contact with the courts and thus start a potential chain reaction of further involvement. The purpose of this chapter has, therefore, been to describe some of the confrontations between the Luke Street boys and the representatives of external authority, and to locate these confrontations in the context of the structural position in which the boys found themselves and the 'views' that this structural position supported. In describing specific incidents an attempt has been made to see the build-up to actions which the outside world regarded as either totally 'senseless' or which in a slightly more enlightened way were regarded as the result of consistently 'anti-social attitudes'. The argument is that it is more profitable to regard the boys' hostile contact with authority as

latent in the situation rather than the individual. We will learn
more about the officially defined delinquent behaviour of
the Luke Street boys by an examination of the position in
which they found themselves and the belief systems operating
on both sides than we will from an examination of the boys'
background characteristics. The 'delinquent' behaviour which
the Luke Street boys were involved in was the product of
their relationship with authority. Although some of them
had been to court on theft charges the more typical cases
were those resulting from their contact with the police. This
kind of 'trouble' became the defining characteristic of the
boys both to themselves and to the people outside the neighbourhood. The only difference was that the boys accurately
saw this 'trouble' as an interaction in which both 'sides' had
a part to play.

It was in their contact with the police that the effects of
the stereotype of Luke Street as being a 'bad' neighbourhood
were at their most extreme. The police were the main group
of 'outsiders' who came into contact with the boys and
although this contact was of an occasional nature it did have
severe effects on the lives of individuals. The police were
in the position of having to maintain law and order and
saw Luke Street and its inhabitants as being particularly
problematic in this respect. Although the police exhibited
a degree of affection for those they regarded as the 'characters'
of the neighbourhood, they also believed that the neighbourhood was productive of general 'trouble'. Luke Street was
the 'worst street in town' and this badness was characterised
by 'trouble'. The police's increased surveillance of the area
and their heightened sensitivity of the possibility of trouble
in the area had a self-fulfilling effect in that they were likely
to interpret behaviour in Luke Street as having the potential
for conflict. In their reaction to the behaviour of the boys the
police made moves which played a part in escalating hostile
contact.

As we have seen, it is difficult to determine 'what happened'
in incidents of the kind described. And this indicates the
importance of subjective interpretations of the incident. The
speed of events makes objective description difficult and
incidents develop not so much in terms of objective situations

but as the result of the meanings attached to those situations. However in a general sense such incidents can be described as the result of the tension on both 'sides' concerning the purpose and action of the other. In the case of the boys it was a belief that the police were in the Luke Street neighbourhood for the purpose of 'unfair' supervision. They held firm views about the rightness or wrongness of the behaviour of groups towards them and this is the key to an understanding of their subjective world and in particular their contact with the police. In these contacts it was always the boys who were 'in the right'. The police on the other hand believed they had a 'job to do' and had to discriminate between behaviour which they considered threatening and behaviour which they did not consider threatening. In Luke Street every fresh incident increased the likelihood of further conflict because the boys' action in relation to the police was the product of the beliefs that these incidents supported. Thus the boys saw the arrival of police in Luke Street as introducing the possibility of an incident. And once an incident had started neither side was prepared to stand down. The feeling that in a sense the police caused the incident was summed up in the statement often heard from both adults and boys in the Luke Street neighbourhood that 'whenever the police come down here there's always trouble'. Thus during my time in Luke Street an impasse seemed to have been arrived at. And the evidence from this study would suggest that the amplificatory consequences of this impasse were severe. In commenting on Wilson and Armstrong's Easterhouse study Cohen has noted that 'the definitions of others are part of the reality of growing up in Easterhouse; it is a problem area, it is a violent area, people are on the look out for violence and certain forms of violence impinge on one's status and are part of the props whereby one builds up one's identity'.[14]

Although the boys had very clear ideas of exactly what the police were allowed to do and what they weren't allowed to do, they realised that in individual confrontations it was more usually a question of two sides and of winning and losing. And in these confrontations it was believed by the boys that the police had the advantage because the courts would always accept their version of 'what happened'. And because of this the boys believed that whatever action they took once they had become involved in the outcome of a particular incident was a matter of chance. It was a question of 'fate' whether the police arrested one boy or another or at its most definite it was a question of one boy or a group of boys being arrested because they were 'known'. Because police power was regarded as indiscriminate the notion that police action might be 'right' was, therefore, discounted.

But although the boys and the police were on opposite 'sides' there was a degree of collusion between the two in terms of the way that they looked at the confrontations in the Luke Street neighbourhood. And this collusion played its part in producing the potential for continuing confrontations. Both groups defined Luke Street as tough and this in itself increased the likelihood of conflict. The police were likely to interpret as aggressive an action which in another neighbourhood might pass as neutral and the boys tended to interpret all police activity as directed against themselves.

To put the various processes and beliefs that were part of the 'incident' into context it is useful to illustrate the dynamics of such an incident by a four-stage description of a typical confrontation in Luke Street:

Stage A Two policeman arrive in the Luke Street neighbourhood.

Stage B The boys realise that they are there. The policeman see the boys and because of their knowledge of other incidents in the area are immediately sensitised to possible conflict.

Stage C Either the police or the boys make the first move in an encounter and this encounter because of the expectations of each side is quickly perceived as a hostile one (for instance, a question by the police is regarded by the boys as 'sticking their noses in where they've got no business' whereas a remark by the boys is regarded as 'cheek' or 'trying them out' by the police.

Stage d A full-scale incident occurs in which the boys regard themselves as being unfairly 'picked on'.

To apportion the 'blame for these incidents in the normal sense is inappropriate. They were the result of sensitivities and stereotypes on the part of both boys and the police. And during the few public seconds that an incident lasted both the boys and the police were the victims of wider processes and beliefs. To the boys' way of thinking it was always the police who 'started' [15] and who were 'interfering where they had no business'. But to the police it was always the boys who made the first move and who tried to stop them doing their lawful duty. If there was 'trouble' or the threat of 'trouble' in Luke Street the police believed they had to be there.

The boys, were, therefore, the victims of a labelling process which was in operation constantly in their daily lives. But it was a labelling process which was not static and took place more in the fluid context of the street than in a specifically organisational context. As a result of the kind of publicity that surrounded the West End and the more general stereotypes that surround unemployed working-class boys, the Luke Street boys found that 'trouble' was expected of them and this had amplificatory consequences in their continuing contact with the police. In analysing delinquent activity it is traditional to talk of opportunity structures. For the Luke Street boys the fact that the outside world associated the denim uniform and hanging about with 'trouble' and a consistently anti-social set of 'attitudes' was part of their opportunity structure.

The Luke Street boys, therefore, regarded themselves as 'blameless' for these incidents. But at the same time their contact with the police became, in their own eyes, one of their defining characteristics. The boys were in the position of having to dispose of time with little money and only very limited access to space. This resulted in the long hours spent hanging about in the public setting of the street – a way of life which can be regarded as entirely normal within the circumstances. Within this unstructured situation they sought some kind of meaning to their lives, and with the absence of any other identity material their contact with the police came to be central to the way in which they viewed their position. The police were literally the only people who took any notice of them and although in terms of actual time the contact was very limited it became significant at a much more general level. Although the boys managed to introduce a degree of variety and style into their daily lives, underlying the way in which they regarded themselves was their confrontation with authority.

In terms of their actual or anticipated contact with the police they saw themselves as being involved in transactions in which each 'side' was in direct oposition to the other. The interests of the police were never the interests of the boys. And in these transactions the boys were aware of the probable sequences of development and of the possible consequences. Certain times and places were regarded as having the potential for conflict and the boys exhibited a degree of insight into the processes that were involved in that conflict.

Wertham notes that 'the gang boy thus aspires to an identity that puts him in a special relationship to risk. When he is around his friends he often creates the situations in which he chooses to exist, an art of creation that involves selecting out certain features of the social environment and then transforming them into conditions that allow him to define a self.'[16] The Luke Street boys were aware that Stage A could lead to Stage B, that Stage B could lead to Stage C and that Stage C could lead to Stage D. In a sense, they put themselves into Stage A in the knowledge that it is likely to lead to Stage D.[17] The appearance of the police in Luke Street was an indication not only that something had happened but also that something would happen. The boys were immediately sensitive to the potential for conflict.

As we have already noted the Luke Street boys were in a position where one of their only courses of action was to make a virtue out of necessity. The identity of being 'outside the law' was one of the few that was readily available to them. And in this fact lies the key to an understanding of the 'trouble' in Luke Street. It also puts into context the fact that was reported to me by several of the boys that they would ring the police and say there was trouble in the area in order to 'draw them down' to Luke Street.

8

TWO MORALITY PLAYS

It's natural.   Eddy

This chapter continues the analysis of 'delinquent' incidents.
Again the focus is on process and the development of subjective interpretations on both 'sides'. Every delinquent act
is unique and has to be analysed on its own terms: and
an understanding of such acts can only be gained by
analysing the interpretations that surround them and giving
a detailed description of 'what happened'. But such acts are
of course interwoven into the continuing lives of the participants and the continuing lives of the groups of which they
are a part.

THE BONFIRE NIGHT RIOTS

This section looks at the 'traditional' bonfire night riots in
the West End which were, to the outside community, perhaps
the most visible indication that the area was a 'delinquent'
one. My intention is to analyse the way in which this tradition
had grown up, the subjective interpretations on both the part
of the boys and the police concerning the nature of the
encounters during the 'riots', and the various moves and
counter-moves that led to the production of an act that was
defined as 'delinquent'. It is shown that the tradition of 'wild'
bonfire nights dated from early 1960s and can thus be linked
with the processes of the social construction of the
neighbourhood. The bonfire night 'riots' were the context
in which both the boys and the police developed the most
extreme interpretations of the situation of conflict. And it
is in this sense that the events can be regarded as local

'morality plays'[1] in which the police came into contact with the boys and expressed their position in extreme terms and the boys came into contact with the police and expressed their position in equally extreme terms. In this analysis I therefore intend to discuss the key aspects of these confrontations: (i) their 'public' nature; (ii) their 'dramatic' quality; (iii) the beliefs operating on both 'sides'.

Bonfire night in the West End was defined as a problematic event. The local police operating on their 'memory file' (the cumulative result of past experiences in the neighbourhood on that night), anticipated conflict and antagonism. As a result they concentrated their resources in the area and expected that there would be antagonistic encounters there. In fact the population of Crossley were subject to a localised 'moral panic' about the possibility of delinquency, rioting and violence on that night in the area and the police would have been seen as failing in their duty had they not anticipated this. The Luke Street boys also anticipated 'trouble' on the night and there was a large influx of other groups into the area for the occasion: and as I shall illustrate, the boys were prepared to let the trouble develop. Thus the key fact is that bonfire night in the West End was anticipated by both sides as a specific time–place context in which trouble and violent encounters were expected to develop. Out of these joint expectations and the active participation of the boys, 'delinquency' was produced and 'delinquent' careers were developed. My analysis of the bonfire night riots is based on discussion with the boys both prior to and after the event, discussions with the police after the event, observations of the event and an analysis of Press reporting of it.

The history of bonfire night in the West End demonstrates one of the themes of this study – that a 'tradition' of 'wildness' had developed in the early to mid–1960s. Bonfire night in the West End was 'traditionally' the night of the year on which there was conflict between the police and the local boys. The number of people arrested in the years prior to my arrival in the Luke Street neighbourhood indicates the strength of this tradition. Press reports of previous bonfire nights indicated that by the late 1960s as many as fifteen people were arrested annually in the area on that night.[2]

Thus by the late 1960s 'trouble' on bonfire night had come to be expected in the West End of town.

Bonfire night in Crossley is traditionally a night of celebration and people are expected to go a little 'wild'. But this is more pronounced in certain parts of the town and the West End, in this respect as in others, had the worst reputation. For instance, in November 1972 the *Crossley News* stated:

> The traditional Crossley bonfire – completely un-authorised and consisting mainly of household rubbish – is slowly dying out according to the town's deputy chief fire officer, Mr — . 'Today they're mainly in certain areas such as the West End' he said. 'Even in the West End' said Mr — 'november 5th was becoming unbearable for residents.'

This general tradition that the West End had large 'illegal' bonfires was recognised by both insiders and outsiders. Some of the long-established residents claimed that: 'Bonfire night has always been rough around our way. Always.' But most of the West Enders were more specific in their dating of the tradition. And the boys in particular pinpointed the date of the beginning of the disturbances to the early 1960s. Frankie thought the bonfires had started getting 'bad' when he was about five years old and Masso said: 'Well, it started about eight years ago. What it was the fire brigade used to come around and take all the stuff. It's grown up since then.' Most of the locals, therefore, dated the beginning of the disturbances to the period that the Luke Street neighbourhood was becoming drawn into the spiral of decline and when 'all the lads' had started 'going wild'. And an element of this traditional aspect was the way in which boys who had moved out of the West End would return for bonfire night because they were 'expecting trouble'.

All the boys when talking about bonfire night agreed that it had got 'really bad'. 'Fire cars won't go in the West End now. One night the lads turned all the fire engines over.' And most of them remembered particularly 'bad' years. Mal for instance thought that 1969 was the worst year and described the scene in Luke Street to me: 'Four years ago last bonfire night there was a big bonfire there. It was a big one. Anyway, there were fire engines, police and everything. You know the lads barricaded the street. And the police got a mechanical shovel and pushed it in.' Mal in fact thought that bonfire night had 'quietened down' in recent years.

O.G. Ever since you've remembered has it been bad on bonfire night?
Mal Well, yes, the last three years have quietened down. But what they used to do which is stupid, you know the — factory, well, they used to go up there and get drums of oil and they'd tip about four over the fire.

Mal also described the detailed plans that were made in the neighbourhood every year in preparation for bonfire night: 'Every bonfire night in the past there was somebody guarding the bommie [bonfire] all night for days before November 5th to make sure it wouldn't be taken by the corporation. And there used to be barricades across the road with people on Casey's roof and the next house in the Dock Road.'[3]

By the early 1970s the tradition of 'wild' bonfire nights in the West End was fully developed. On the basis of field-notes taken immediately after the event I want to describe the first bonfire during my time in Luke Street. To put the events of the evening into perspective it is necessary to recognise the build-up of activity in the previous days. Tensions and expectations were rising. Bonfire material had been collected and stockpiled in the disused flats in Cambridge Square and attempts had been made by the police and the fire brigade to remove it. Some of the local residents had put wire grills over their front windows in anticipation of the 'rioting'. The local club, the Pembroke, was closed for the night and the youth leader had spent the afternoon covering the windows with steel plates. The events of the evening were as follows.

6.30 p.m.
The bonfire, unlike in the afternoon, was now in position

in the lower half of Cambridge Square. It was approximately twenty feet high. There was a group of about fifty fourteen-to eighteen-year-old boys in the square standing beside the bonfire. A group of younger children were also there on the fringe of this group. Everything was fairly quiet. The boys were just 'standing around'. There were no girls in the square and very few adults, although there was activity on the balconies with families out watching the 'goings on'. I stayed in the square with the group for about ten minutes and got talking to Robbie. He wasn't a member of the main group but was accepted and knew what would happen. He seemed keen to give me a preview of the events of the evening, show me around and act as my guarantor. Robbie's personal attitude to the evening's events was that although he didn't intend to get into any trouble himself he felt it was important to be around when 'anything' happened and didn't want to miss the evening's events. At the end of the evening he expanded on this and told me that although he had no intention or desire to get into 'trouble' he was keen to 'run with'[4] the leaders. Robbie was able to give me an accurate outline of what would happen. He said that as in previous years everything had been planned and that there would definitely be contact with the police at one stage of the evening. He said that the bonfire in the square wouldn't be lit until after eight o'clock but that the other bonfire behind Casey's would be lit before that. After the Luke Street bonfire had died down the group would then return to the square and at about nine o'clock the main events of the evening would begin.

7.30 p.m.

Like everybody else we then began to move down out of the square towards Luke Street. Several boys were left to guard the bonfire in the square. Behind Casey's another bonfire, about as large as the square one, had now been built. The entrance to Luke Street was covered with rubbish and broken bottles and there was material in position for a barricade. The same group of about fifty boys had arrived from the square and they were joined by others. We all stood around waiting for the bonfire to be lit. There was more

general activity in Luke Street than there had been in the
square and some of the Luke Street families were standing
in the front gardens. Several of these families had attempted
to have their own more conventional firework display but
these were short-lived and didn't detract from the central
focus of the street – the bonfire and the large group of boys
around it. There were more girls in evidence in Luke Street
then there had been in the square but they were standing
together in excited groups in the front gardens rather than
in the street itself.

8.00 p.m.

The first sign of contact with the police came when a police
car drove very fast down Luke Street. But on coming around
the corner to try to get out into the Dock Road the car was
confronted with the rubble and forced to brake hard. It
stopped for a few seconds but the driver didn't open the
door. The car reversed equally rapidly up Luke Street. When
the car arrived in the street there was some shouting from the
younger members of our group, although the older ones
seemed to be 'waiting to see what happened'. But as it moved
back some of the boys followed it and a chant of 'A-g-g-r-O,
A-g-g-r-o, A-g-g-r-o', began.

8.15 p.m.

The Luke Street bonfire was lit and burned for about twenty
minutes with nothing eventful happening except some of the
boys throwing bangers at each other. By the time this fire
had died down and the main group, which was now about
100 strong, began to move up to Cambridge Square where
it was joined by other groups so that there were about 200
boys aged from about thirteen to twenty in the square. Again
there were no girls in the square but along with a lot of
family groups, they were watching from the balconies.

8.45 p.m.

The main bonfire was lit and everybody waited for about
fifteen minutes. Then Robbie told me me 'it' was about to

begin and that the 'big lads' were preparing to go up to the top section of the square. The whole group of two hundred, myself and Robbie included, moved slowly through the square in an extended line and stopped in the top section. From this position six of the 'big lads' detached themselves from our main group and ran up to the corner of Pembroke Street and threw a brick through a private house window opposite the youth club. A group of police were standing on the opposite corner but they did nothing. Our group continued throwing bottles from the narrow entrance of Cambridge Square for about ten minutes. Bricks and bottles were thrown at cars going round the roundabout. A bus was stoned as it passed the entrance to the square. A panda car drove very fast around the roundabout and the group threw bricks and bottles at it. By this time a crowd of about forty local residents had gathered outside the square on the corner of Pembroke Road. On the other side of Pembroke Road, out of range of missiles, a group of about seven police were now standing in a group. Big Jim, the police constable, detached himself from this group and walked towards the entrance of the square. When he got within firing range our group let loose another volley of bricks and bottles. There were chants of 'Jim Jones, Jim Jones'. But Big Jim walked on to the entrance of the square and began talking to some of our group. After five minutes other police followed him until there were about five police at the entrance to the square. None of the police followed and they returned to their corner of Pembroke Road. During this time of reassessment (above ten minutes) small groups of about four or five detached themselves and ran quickly up to the entrance of the flats, threw bricks and bottles at passing cars, and then returned immediately to the main group.

9.35 p.m.

The core of the 'big lads' then decided to change the offensive and we all left the square by a side entrance and ran into Cambridge Road. We ran up and down the road from the Dock Road to the square and passing cars were stoned. A double decker bus came up Cambridge Road and its passage

was blocked by about half the group. It was forced to a
standstill and a brick was thrown through one of the ground
floor windows. The bus moved forward through our group
and we went back to the bottom of Cambridge Road. Bricks
were thrown through some of the windows of houses in
Cambridge Road. One woman in her forties rushed out
shouting 'I know who did it, I know who did it' and proceeded
to go after him.

9.55 p.m.

By this time the police had apparently decided that 'something would have to be done'. From their position on the
corner of Pembroke Road a police van with about eight
policemen in it (the main group of police had now increased
to possibly twenty-five or thirty, with four or five panda cars
and jeeps) drove very fast down Cambridge Road. It was
stoned and bottled. It braked quickly at the bottom of
Cambridge Road and leaving two policemen in the van the
remaining six jumped out and caught hold of anybody they
could. Five of our group were pulled into the van. From
observation it was simply the only five of the group they
could catch. I saw only one of the five throw a brick at
the police van. During this charge myself and three or four
others were chased up Cambridge Road by a policeman.
We finally stopped and said we were 'allowed to be out
on the street' and that we hadn't thrown anything. In return
we were told to 'scram' to 'get off the streets' or else we'd
be 'taken in'. Although I didn't witness them there were
other police charges while this was taking place and all
in all fourteen people were arrested. By about eleven o'clock
the area was quiet. For approximately two and a half hours –
the duration of the conflict with the police – I had been with
the group and like the majority of the group had simply
been 'running with the big lads'. Perhaps less than twenty
of the boys had actually thrown anything.

This then is a description of the main events of bonfire
night. It is useful to distinguish two aspects of these disturbances for further analysis – their purpose or meaning to

the boys involved and their outcome in terms of their becoming part of the internal 'consciousness' of the area and the external definition of the area.

The 'purpose' of the bonfire night disturbance is, of course, linked with its traditional aspects. Many of the boys who were involved in the disturbances on bonfire night were there because 'trouble' was expected and even if they did not want to instigate or participate in that 'trouble' directly they certainly wanted to be 'around' when it happened.[5] This was not only because of the intrinsic excitement and movement that a clash with the police offered but also because to be in the Cambridge Square – Luke Street part of Crossley on bonfire night and to be prepared to run with the group was a very clear indication of what 'side' one was on. The group allegiances of the Luke Street boys could best be understood in terms of a heirarchy of loyalties. And it was on bonfire night and during the other occasional large-scale group disturbances that the 'extended loyalties' of the group were most apparent. Individual groups come together under the general definition of 'lads from the West End' and were bound together for the duration of the disturbances in terms of their relationship with an equally clearly defined adversary – the police.

In terms of the subjective meanings of the incidents the locational and territorial aspect of the disturbances is also of significance. The way in which the boys talked about the events indicated that they were associated with the outside world impinging its authority on the area. The boys' belief that the West End was the 'wildest part' of town and Luke Street was the 'worst street in Crossley' was closely linked to the idea of the tradition of bonfire night disturbances. It is too exaggerated to suggest that the boys were defending their territory in any direct and obvious sense, and yet the perceived conflict between the neighbourhood and the outside world was very obvious from the way in which the boys talked about bonfire night. Besides highlighting the themes of group identity and territoriality the bonfire night disturbances were often attributed with specific meanings by both the participants and local residents generally. The most commonly expressed of these was the idea that bonfire night

was the time when 'the lads got their own back' as a group
on those people who had 'got at them' individually during
the year. In particular the disturbances were seen as the boys'
way of getting back at individual cases of police discrimination in the previous year. For instance I was told that
'false arrests are stored up and the police pay the price
on bonfire night'.

Much of what the boys said also indicated that the
disturbances could be explained in terms of the victims of
the attacks being chosen. The picture put forward in the local
Press was that the disturbances were unpremeditated and
unplanned. Indeed their use of the word 'riot' suggests
turmoil and lack of co-ordination. But viewed from the
inside, not only were the bonfire night disturbances accurately
anticipated but also their victims were chosen. And those
victims were always outsiders. As one of the boys' elder
brothers said: 'It's never local people that get hurt. It's only
policemen and firemen and the likes of them.'

Whether or not the intended victims did in fact suffer during
the short confrontations is doubtful but certainly the 'talk'
relating to bonfire night indicated this planning aspect.
During my time in Luke Street the past events or future
anticipations of bonfire night were a relatively frequent topic
of conversation. And the 'talk' relating to bonfire night,
besides indicating a general hostility – 'anybody with any
money gets their shop done on bommie night' – also indicated the boys' desire to 'get their own back' on individuals
involved in sending their members to court. This was illustrated in the mid-May following the bonfire night reported in
these pages when Rappo had been sent to Borstal. We were
walking away from the court and talking about the shop-
owner who had given evidence against Rappo. The boys
suggested that 'next bommie her windows are definitely going
in'.

The 'logic' of the bonfire night disturbances was also
illustrated by the tradition that certain premises were attacked
during the evening every year. Talking about previous bonfire
nights the boys indicated that the Pembroke Club was usually
the building to suffer most. And as I have said, the leader
of the club anticipated this tradition every year by boarding

up his premises and closing the club. As we have seen, the club was unpopular with the Luke Street boys, who resented the way in which they believed that the leader restricted membership to the club in terms of 'suitable' addresses. This was in fact the reason that the boys usually gave for the first bonfire night attack on the club. For instance Masso told me: 'Every bommie night the Pemmie gets done in and you know why it is, it's because he don't let any of Cambridge Square in.'

In looking at the individual events that taken together make up the bonfire night disturbances it is important to distinguish between two central elements in terms of the impact that they had on their participants: first the inherent excitement that the disturbances offered and second the high degree of resentment that was felt about police activity on the evening. The excitement aspect was evident not only from the way in which the boys anticipated the event, but also from the way in which it was described afterwards. The drama, the controlled and purposeful 'going off our heads' and the element of contest were central factors in the way the boys thought about the events of bonfire night. Possibly the best way to conceptualise these incidents is in terms of their *movement*. The intense activity, the moves and the counter-moves and the speed with which the events occurred are all important for an understanding of their significance for the boys concerned. Also of course it must be remembered that the events in the Luke Street neighbourhood that were regarded by the outside world as spontaneous 'riots' and 'attacks' had in fact been planned, to the extent that the boys were not only in the right place at the right time and with the right equipment but also could anticipate the probable sequence of events. In the bonfire night disturbances the tradition of conflict with the police was important but for that tradition to be activated group planning was necessary. The boys not only knew that they would come together on that night but could also fairly accurately anticipate the probable sequence of events and the consequences of their action. Furthermore this element of planning is significant not only in terms of the actual events themselves but also for the intrinsic excitement that the process of planning offered and the opportunities that it provided for individual boys to show very clearly which side they were on. Both individual boys and the group as a whole were in a position in which there was no direct need for them to have been involved in the events described. But they exhibited a degree of insight into the process by which the events could develop and were therefore in a position to choose whether or not to become involved in that process. In concrete terms the choice for individual boys in terms of initiating conflict was at the level of where to 'hang about', when to 'hang about' and whom to 'hang about' with. The combination of a certain location at a certain time and with certain companions had the potential for 'trouble' and the boys were aware of this. To be in the centre of Cambridge Square on bonfire night indicated a certain readiness to be involved in trouble. The fact that people travelled from other areas into the West End on bonfire night is a clear indication of this.

But at the same time the police methods of apprehension on bonfire night as at other times caused resentment. The police were in a position in which they were forced to use their discretion and the boys believed that police methods were arbitrary; this had important effects on the feelings of group solidarity – 'we're all in it together' – because anybody by just being there could be 'pulled in'. Frankie for instance when asked how the police arrested people out of a large group like on bonfire night said: 'They just go into the middle and get any cunt they can lay their hands on.'[6]

The following is part of a taped conversation about bonfire night between Brown and Eddy:

Brown They had Lombo and got him out of the garden.
Eddy What they said was that they were going to make the West End pay for the damage they'd done over the year. We wouldn't mind if they got roped in for something they done.[7] But they were coming down in vans and just pulling in everybody in the road. An eight-year-old lad and they say he assaulted a six-foot copper . . .
Brown The police said to him on bommie night 'come here you, you fuzzy headed bastard'.
Eddy I went to court for bommie night. First charge he

had me up for, Disorderly Behaviour and Breach of the Peace and Abusive Language. First of all we went up Monday, then it got adjourned to the next week. But it got adjourned again. We went up the third week. The third week this copper comes up and says 'I want you' he takes me down to the cells. He says 'I'm charging you.' So I says 'What the hell for' and he says assault. So I say who've I assaulted. He says me, you hit me over the head with a bottle. So I didn't say nothing. So he says have you got anything to say, so I says no. I tell him whatever he's got to say write it down I'm going to court any case. So he gets in the court and says I was standing at the corner of Cambridge Road and threw a bottle at him. So that's when I got three months and — got three months and he'd never done a bloody thing. Someone had threatened he was going to get his house smashed in so he was standing there waiting. And . . . he was standing between his parents, so this jeep comes up and a copper gets out and says you get in this fucking wagon an' all. He says what have I done, and his parents ran at them and says he hasn't done nothing. The police said he fucking has, and so they put him the van and put the bracelets on him. In the van he goes to open the back door and says look at this lads and the copper says look at this and smacks him in the face. He was crying and everything. They were just going round roping everybody in. They even pulled an old fellow in. There was a little gang of kids about ten years old outside Casey's so this bloody copper comes round in a panda, and gives one of the kids a belt in the face. So — says leave the fucking kids alone. He was just going into the pub. Well he got pulled up for drunk and disorderly behaviour. He got three months in — [local prison].

The bonfire disturbances described in this section were given extensive Press coverage which increased the stereotype of the lawlessness of the area. The local paper reported:

STONES FLY AS CROSSLEY MOB RUNS RIOT

A dazed Crossley started to clear the mess today from

last night's Bonfire night riots in the West End of the town when a mob of 400[8] ran riot . . . looking more like Belfast than Crossley, the mob stoned everything that moved in the Cambridge Square area . . .

The analogy with Belfast was made repeatedly in the following weeks as the arrested boys appeared in court. Three weeks later the major local paper carried the report:

BONFIRE NIGHT SCENE WAS JUST LIKE BELFAST

Screaming Bonfire night hordes of teenagers surrounded a bus, hurled bricks through its windows, threw bottles and other missiles, including metal, at the police and went bersek, it was alleged at Crossley Magistrates Court today. 'I'm not stretching a point when I say it was exactly the same as you see in Belfast on the television, it was shocking' said Inspector — .

During the same week there were further reports headed 'BONFIRE NIGHT LIKE BELFAST' and 'POLICE STONED IN BELFAST-TYPE RIOT' which all referred to the police inspector's description of the events as being like those in Belfast. In terms of press coverage it is interesting that the implicit suggestion was that the adults of the neighbourhood were in collusion with the boys. The local paper, for instance, reported: 'The disturbances attracted spectators who stood on street corners to watch the confrontation between the police and troublemakers. Some had even brought boxes to sit on to watch the spectacle.'

These examples of Press reports indicate the way in which the occasional disturbances in the West End were viewed and reported in the local Press. And the characteristics of the disturbances themselves were used to put forward the stereotype of the West End in ever more extreme terms. The events of bonfire night both activated and developed the belief that the West End of town was the 'worst part of Crossley', that it had a 'hard core' in the Cambridge Square and Luke Street area and that in the West End the problems of adolescent delinquency and vandalism were extreme. In

addition to this the actual events of bonfire night were interpreted in such a way as to extend the stereotypes already in
existence. The belief that what had happened was 'senseless'
and 'meaningless' was implicit in the Press reports and so also
was the idea that the events were *disorganised*. The picture
suggested was that of a lack of internal control in the area;
that because of the kinds of people they were, even a night
which was meant to be an enjoyable celebration would naturally turn into a night of destruction; that the group would
change into a 'mob' and the celebrations into 'riots'. Added
to this the factual events of the evening were exaggerated.
Press reports, for example, referred to the boys 'ripping up
pavements to use as ammunition'.

The end result of the bonfire night disturbances described
in this section was the appearance in court of twelve of the
fourteen originally arrested. Two of these were aged fifteen
and twelve, and they therefore appeared before the Juvenile
Court. Of the remaining ten, one was aged 39, one was 20
and one was 19, three were 18, four were seventeen. All ten
pleaded not guilty on various grounds such as simply not
being in the group but walking past, being in the group but
watching not throwing, or trying to stop other members of
the group damaging their houses. Two of the ten were
acquitted because of lack of evidence, four were sent to
detention centres for three months and three were fined £50
each. The thirty-nine-year-old man was sent to prison for
three months. Both the court case and the sentences themselves caused resentment amongst the boys and other
residents of the area. Particular resentment was felt about the
thirty-nine-year-old man and his case became one of the
'stories' of the area often used in conversations as evidence of
police discrimination. It was repeated to me by both the boys
and adults in the neighbourhood a considerable time after
the event.

To conclude this section on the bonfire night 'riots' it
is necessary to be more specific about the role of the police.
I do not wish to argue that because the police are the initial
definers of delinquency there would be no delinquency if
the police had not been in Luke Street on bonfire night.
To throw a brick through a bus window is an illegal act

and is recognised as such by the individuals involved. But I do wish to argue that the presence of a large number of police in the area not only had the effect of defining the context as highly problematic and thus raising on all sides the expectations of problematic behaviour but also that their presence focused the action of the boys and therefore structured the form that delinquency took. In talking about police work it is usual to talk of tensions and contradictions. One such contradiction is that the police are expected to control trouble but their presence may exacerbate and amplify such trouble. The high level of discretion that the police used in the individual encounters also meant that their role can be interpreted in terms of assigning particular members of the group to the role of vandal or delinquent. The 'opposing sides' were therefore visible and trouble developed out of the expectations that each had of the other. Once again the boys' subjective interpretation was that the police were 'out to get them' and for the police the boys were the local 'folk devils' whose behaviour had to be stamped out.

THE 'ATTACKS' ON CASEY'S

This section focuses on the 'attacks' on Casey's which occurred after the pub was taken over by a new landlord. These attacks occurred soon after my arrival in Luke Street and for the whole of my time there remained one of the 'stories' of Luke Street. The story was referred to by the boys as an example of a 'victorious' delinquent encounter and by outsiders as characterising the 'kind of behaviour you expect down there'. The role of the police in these encounters was not so central as in the incidents on the street or in the bonfire night 'riots'. But the police action was of significance in developing the boys' perspectives on the problematic nature of the situation. Again the role of the local Press was of significance in highlighting the 'dramatic' quality of the encounters and further defining it as a highly problematic situation.

Before describing the actual 'attacks' on the pub it is necessary to re-emphasise the significance that Casey's and the corner had for the boys. They were, as we have already seen, very limited in terms of their access to space; Casey's and the corner outside it was their meeting point. Any action that jeopardised what they regarded as 'their' corner was therefore likely to have repercussions. And in fact the encounters described below can be interpreted, from the boys point of view, as a logical outcome of the attempt to move them away from the corner.

The new landlord came to Casey's four months after the 'Misfits' report had been produced and there was a high degree of sensitivity in the neighbourhood about the actions and beliefs of outsiders. His general unpopularity and the attacks on the pub made by the boys forced him to leave within two months. The events leading up to his departure indicated the hostility felt in the neighbourhood by both adults and adolescents against an outsider who was not only thought to be 'using'[9] local people but also to be trying to impose his own particular values for his own particular ends and to be trying to 'change things'. To be more specific the new landlord's initial unpopularity can be attributed to three factors: (i) he was unpopular with the Casey's regulars because he raised the price of beer and gained a reputation for short-changing customers; (ii) he gave local residents the impression that he thought he was 'superior' to them; (iii) on his arrival at Casey's he made it clear that he intended to 'tame' the neighbourhood as he was reported to have done in his previous pub in another town.

One of the first actions that the new landlord took was to ban the young children in the area coming to the bar. As there were no shops that stayed open late in the area it had been traditional for Casey's to keep a stock of sweets and soft drinks and to allow children into the bar to buy them. In fact up until the arrival of the new landlord it was not unusual to see children of seven or eight coming into the bar up until closing time and buying sweets. The ban on children caused resentment locally as the children not only went into the bar to buy sweets but also to 'get messages' for their parents. The resentment became far greater when there was an incident concerning Rappo's use of the phone (again the phone in Casey's was the only available public phone in Luke Street as the nearby ones had been 'vandalised'); the landlord decided to ban everybody under eighteen and anybody who had a 'skinhead'. As Mal said at the time: 'It was —'s fault. He started off by stopping the little kids going in to buy sweets. Then he banned Rappo from it. That's when the trouble really began.'

Here Jimmy describes the telephone incident and the ensuing ban on anybody wearing the skinhead uniform:

The trouble really started when he came, you know, — , the tenant of the pub. When he first came he banned the skinheads for no reason at all. He said they were under age which was all wrong. Like on one incident – I was there – and Rappo produced a birth certificate to say he was eighteen. That's the night he snatched the telephone out of his hand when he was talking. He said he wasn't eighteen. But he was eighteen. Up to then the kids were all going into Casey's. They weren't causing any trouble. Just playing records. He banned everybody who looked like a skinhead, had a denim jacket and short hair. It was as simple as that.

The banning of the skinheads and other locals associated with them was also given as the main reason for the trouble by Eddy: 'A lad came into Casey's one afternoon, you know he works on the bins and he was dirty, you know he'd been working. Well, the lad just puts his foot up on the chair and Johnny has him banned for that.' It was not simply the fact of banning the skinheads that caused resentment. Equally important was the new landlord's perceived 'attitude':

Jacko He came from a pub in — saying I'll tame these Crossley bastards. He was telling everybody what he was going to do in Crossley. He came in with the attitude it's supposed to be be tough around here is it, well I'll fucking show them.

His 'attitude' and the ban on the skinheads led to the beginning of trouble in Casey's and on the corner:

Jacko As soon as he starts banning then he got fucking done.
We put all the windows in, painted all over the walls.

The actual attacks on the pub occurred over a number
of days. Stones and bricks were thrown at the windows and
damage was done inside the pub to the toilets and jukebox.
At this stage in the proceedings the police began to patrol
the area with increased intensity. As a police spokesman said
in a Press report specifically in relation to the attacks: 'this
is a rough area and it keeps getting its windows put in.
Every time there's an incident we go there.' In fact the landlord made frequent calls to the police about the behaviour
of the banned skinheads:

Eddy He started ordering us about – get off the corner and
all this. He used to phone the dixies [police] if we were
just on the corner.

The conflict between the banned skinheads and the landlord increased in intensity and a number of incidents followed. The boys located the place about quarter of a mile away
where he parked his expensive car and sprayed it with paint.
An attempt was made to break down the front door of the
pub. In the final major incident which led to the temporary
closure of Casey's a drum of paint was lit by the boys and
rolled into the bar. As a result of the attacks the landlord
took renewed precautions to protect his pub. The brewery
sign was removed, the bar windows had heavy steel plates
put over them and the first floor windows were fitted with
protective wire covers. This along with the paint and the
additional graffiti which appeared on the walls of Casey's
during the attacks gave the pub a particularly forbidding
appearance resulting in such remarks from the locals as
'welcome to San Quentin'.
    The attacks on Casey's were of course a talking point in
the neighbourhood – particularly amongst the men who
drank there regularly. There was a degree of support from
the older men for the boys' action arising from the general
unpopularity of the landlord. Also it is instructive to look
at the way in which the older men interpreted this delin-

quency. Many of the locals asked 'what can you expect if he treats them like that', and one of the major interpretations offered locally for delinquency was the 'environmental argument'. Many locals believed that delinquency was the result of a lack of facilities in the area and therefore if the one facility that the boys did have – Casey's – was denied to them it was 'logical' that there would be 'trouble'.

The attacks on Casey's, like the bonfire night disturbances, attracted Press coverage. Frequent Press reports of the events not only increased the hostility of the local boys towards the landlord, but also enhanced the excitement and the 'dramatic' quality of the attacks themselves. They also made it necessary for the police to be seen to be 'doing something' about the situation. All the local papers carried reports of the attacks which characterised the landlord as the upright citizen battling against the forces of deviance:

PUB TERRORISED BY BANNED YOUTHS

A Crossley licensee claims he is the victim of a campaign of terror organised by gangs of youths he has banned from his dockland pub . . . The youths have been stoning the New Commercial public house in Dock Road, Crossley, and have even hurled burning oil drums and timber at the doors and windows. — took the pub on . . . He says he had fond memories of it from many years ago when there was a bowling green and football pitch alongside. The present circumstances there are far worse than he ever imagined, and although the customers are mainly ordinary working men, the vandalism outside is 'making his life hell'.

Other reports referred to Casey's as 'kept under seige by gangs of up to 15 youths and girls'. This reporting of the events caused resentment amongst the older people in the area. To quote Jimmy again:

He got pictures taken by the [national paper] to show how good he was. He had a picture of a gallon drum of paint and all these stones. He had them on the bar and everyone who came in he was showing them to. But little did they know he was robbing them left right and centre on the prices. He put the price of ale up when he came there. He said it was because of the vandalism. He was in — [paper]. The people in the area took it all as an insult. This fellow was running everyone down. At one stage like he had half the people leave the pub altogether. They just couldn't put up with him and his sarcastic remarks.

Within four months of his arrival at Casey's, the landlord left and this again was widely reported. The following report for instance links the events with the original 'misfit business':

— QUITS PUB

Four months of non-stop terror by dockside thugs have finally forced — to quit the pub he took over in a bid to disprove claims that the waterfront in Crossley is populated by the drop-outs.

After his departure Casey's was taken over by a landlady, who was immediately as popular as her predecessor had been unpopular. Her popularity could be attributed not only to her re-allowing the Luke Street boys to use Casey's and listen to the jukebox but more directly to her 'attitude'. She had lived locally and relations with the Casey's regulars were immediately friendly. The episode came to a close with the landlady quoted in the *Crossley News* as saying that 'you treat people right and they'll treat you right back'. And her 'attitude' was well recognised by the Casey's regulars who described her as 'treating us like human beings', and told her that if any more windows were broken they would have a whip round and get them replaced. The grills were taken off the windows and life in Casey's returned to normal. But for at least one person, a local boy who received a three months' sentence in a detention centre for his part in the attacks, the episode did not have such a satisfactory ending.

DELINQUENT EVENTS AND NEIGHBOURHOOD IDENTITY

This chapter has attempted to show not only what was

happening during the incidents described but also how the behaviour of different people on different 'side' was inter-related to produce a 'delinquent' event or sequence. In doing this, it may seem that situations which are unique, extreme and not typical of the behaviour normally classified as delinquent have been dealt with in an over-detailed fashion. But all 'delinquent' acts are in some sense unique and the incidents described in this chapter were exactly the sort that led to Luke Street boys being fined, put on proba-tion and sent away. And the description of these incidents suggests not only that they were less extreme than the sensa-tionalised Press reports claimed but also that they took place very quickly and that it was not only behaviour on the part of the boys that was problematic. Although the two events described in this chapter were obviously not identical they had underlying similarities in terms of structure and their effects on the neighbourhood. The most important of these similarities was in their logical development, their dramatic quality, their emphasis on the territorial and locational aspects of conflict and the interpretations of 'what happened' being different for 'insiders' and 'outsiders', with each set of interpretations moving towards internal consistency. The description of these two events highlights, therefore, some of the main characteristics of the conflict with authority that the boys found themselves involved in. And a central task is to examine both the way in which the events become part of the internal conciousness of the neighbourhood and the way in which they were interpreted by the outside world. The events described in this chapter not only developed the perceptions of the existence of two hostile worlds but they resulted from definitions and expectations already held. Thus their role can be seen as a crystallisation and concretisation of understandings. A key characteristic of the events, therefore, was that they were public. They were public not only in the sense that they were observable but also in the more general sense that they became part of the verbal tradition of the area. And because of this tradition long periods could go by without an incident but there was still the conciousness that in certain circumstances certain conflicts would be openly exhibited.

In the case of the bonfire night disturbances and the attacks on Casey's the incidents became part of the external as well as the internal consciousness of the area. The outside world gained a knowledge of the events and again there was a process of amplification. Because of the lack of actual contact between the internal and the external worlds the local Press played an important part. Events such as the bonfire night disturbances and the attacks on Casey's were described in sensationalised detail in the Press and this became part of the public definition of the neighbourhood. The events were also described in such a way as to develop and produce the stereotype of a state of hostility existing between the neighbourhood and 'all right thinking people'. Local press comparisons between the West End and Belfast increased these locational definitions. There was thus a feedback from the incident on the street to the public consciousness of the neighbourhood. And this feedback produced a generalised picture. The individual event which might have been quite untypical in terms of a sample of behaviour in Luke Street came to be taken externally as commonplace and as exemplifying the key characteristics of the neighbourhood. There was thus a feeling that 'that's the kind of behaviour you expect in Luke Street'. Through a process of circular reinforcement the perception of a relationship of hostility was increased on both sides. Luke Street became further isolated from the outside world.

9

LUKE STREET IN COURT

They're as thick as thieves down there.
                    Clerk of Crossley magistrates court

This study is concerned with events at a neighbourhood level rather than the way in which individuals were processed through the local court system. It is however necessary to describe the role of the courts and the boys' subjective experience of them in as much as these institutions legally defined their behaviour as delinquent. In doing so they stabilised or developed 'delinquent' careers. In the court behaviour which was the result of complex patterns of inter-action between the boys and authority was interpreted in a concrete and uni-dimensional fashion. The boys were abstracted from their social context and the pressures and processes of that context and dealt with as *individuals* with 'anti-social attitudes' who were involved in self-determined delinquent activity. The courtroom transactions therefore marked the final registration stage in the social production of delinquent behaviour in Luke Street.

This chapter is divided into three sections. In the first section I analyse the legal sanctions imposed on the Luke Street residents generally and then look specifically at the sanctions imposed on the boys. In the second section I discuss the boys' subjective experience of the court. And in the third section I concentrate on the courtroom transactions that surrounded the delinquent 'incidents' in which the boys had been involved. The analysis is based on the official crime statistics made available to me by the local criminal records office, conversations with the boys and other Luke Street residents, and my own personal observations of approximately twenty-five cases in which boys from the area were involved.[1]

LEGAL SANCTIONS IMPOSED

The legal sanctions imposed on the residents of Luke Street are presented in Tables 9.1–9.4. As in Chapter 3 these are broken down into four groups: (i) males born before 1945; (ii) females born before 1945; (iii) males born after 1945; (iv) females born after 1945. The four cases in the tables in which there is no record of legal sanctions (males born after 1945 cases 5 and 31, females born after 1945 cases 7 and 10) were cases in which the individuals concerned had been given absolute or conditional discharges on all convictions. The category of 'other' includes disqualified from driving, binding over to keep the peace and in one case committal to a mental hospital. Sentences of imprisonment or Borstal training to run concurrent are not included in the tables but Borstal 'recalls' are included. Social services supervision orders and care of local authority cases are only included for post-1945 cases. As in Chapter 3 it should be noted that these

Table 9.1

Legal sanctions imposed (males born before 1945)

Case no.	Fined	Probation	Attendance centre	Approved school	Detention centre	Borstal	Imprisonment	Imprisonment (suspended)	Other
1		1							
2	1	5	1				5		
3	2	5		1				1	
4	4						1		
5	2	2					4		
6	2	2	1				3		
7	1								
8	2								
9	2	2		1					
10								1	
11	3	1							
12	1								
13	3	1					1		
14	1	1							
15							2		
16	4	2			1	1			
17								1	

tables include some cases that occurred after the end of the full-time research period, and also that I consider the information supplied to me was an under-estimate of the number of charges and resulting sanctions concerning residents of the area.

Table 9.2

Legal sanctions imposed (females born before 1945)

Case no.	Fined	Probation	Attendance centre	Approved school	Detention centre	Borstal	Imprisonment	Imprisonment (suspended)	Other
1	1								
2	1								
3									1
4		1							
5		1							
6	1								
7	2								
8	1								
9	2								

The tables indicate that a significant proportion of the Luke Street residents had experienced the range of sanctions that the courts can impose. Analysing these records made it apparent that some of the residents in the area had experienced the typical and depressing cumulative list of sanctions. This point can be illustrated by two actual cases:

Case 1   (males born after 1945)
            Age 10   Probation 12 months
            Age 12   Attendance centre 12 hours
            Age 12   Probation 2 years
            Age 13   28 days remand home
            Age 15   Approved school
            Age 18   Fined £20
            Age 22   9 months imprisonment
            Age 23   28 days detention
            Age 25   18 months imprisonment

Table 9.3

Legal sanctions imposed (males born after 1945)

Case no.	Fined	Supervision order (local authority)	Care of local authority	Probation	Attendance centre	Approved school	Detention centre	Borstal	Imprisonment	Imprisonment (suspended)	Other
1	1			2	1	1	1	1	2		1
2	1			2							
3	1			3		2		1			
4	1			2	2	1					
5											
6	1										
7	5			2	1			1	2		
8		1	1								
9	1										1
10	1						1		1	1	
11				1						1	
12	4			1			1	1	2	1	
13		1			1						
14	3		1					2			
15				1				1	1		
16		1									
17	4										
18				2	1	1	1				
19	3			1		1					
20	1			1			1				
21	1	1			1						
22	3						3				
23	3							1			
24	4			1	2	1	1	2			
25	2	1									
26	4				1		1				
27	1										
28				2							
29	1										
30	1		3					2		1	
31											
32				2							
33	1										
34	2										
35	2			1			1			1	
36	2		1		1		1	2	1	1	
37	3			2			1	1			
38	3			2	1		1	1			

Table 9.4

Legal sanctions imposed (females born after 1945)

Case no.	Fined	Supervision order (local authority)	Care of local authority	Probation	Attendance centre	Approved school	Detention centre	Borstal	Imprisonment	Imprisonment (suspended)	Other
1	1			2							
2	1			1							
3				1							
4				1							
5				1							
6	1										
7											
8	3			2							
9		1									
10											
11	1										
12		1									
13	1										
14	6		1	3		1					

Case 2   (males born after 1945)

       Age 13   Probation 2 years
       Age 14   Fined £1
       Age 14   Attendance centre 24 hours
       Age 14   Fined £2
       Age 14   Attendance centre 24 hours
       Age 15   Approved school
       Age 16   Fined £5
       Age 17   Detention centre 3 months
       Age 18   Borstal training
       Age 19   Recalled to Borstal training
       Age 19   Fined £1

From the records made available to me it was also possible to analyse the sanctions imposed on seven of the group of nine 'boys on Casey's corner' for whom records existed. For the purposes of anonymity these individual cases, as in Chapter 5, are again presented in random order:

Case 1   Age 17 Fined £10
              Age 19 3 months detention centre
              Age 21 9 months imprisonment
              Age 21 6 months imprisonment (suspended)

Case 2   Age 15 Fined £20
              Age 16 Attendance centre 24 hours
              Age 18 3 months detention centre
              Age 19 Fined £25

Case 3   Age 19 Fined £25

Case 4   Age 15 Probation 2 years
              Age 17 Detention centre 3 months
              Age 18 Borstal training
              Age 19 Fined £2
              Age 20 Fined £5
              Age 20 Imprisonment 6 months (suspended)

Case 5   Age 12 Fined £2
              Age 12 Probation 2 years
              Age 13 Attendance centre 24 hours
              Age 14 Fined £2
              Age 16 Care of local authority
              Age 17 Detention centre 3 months
              Age 17 Borstal training
              Age 19 Borstal recall
              Age 19 3 months imprisonment (suspended)
              Age 19 3 months imprisonment

Case 6   Age 13 Probation 2 years
              Age 15 Fined £2
              Age 15 Probation 2 years
              Age 16 Detention centre 3 months
              Age 17 Fined £2
              Age 17 Borstal training
              Age 18 Fined £25

Case 7   Age 14 Probation 2 years
              Age 15 Attendance centre 24 hours

Age 16　Fined £10
Age 17　Detention centre 6 months
Age 17　Probation 2 years
Age 17　Fined £10
Age 17　Fined £20
Age 18　Borstal training

The group of boys on whom I have based the ethnographic detail in this study had therefore come into personal contact with the sanctions that society utilises to control, dissuade, punish, reform and help the individual transgressor. In analysing these individual records one further important point needs to be made. In this study I have focused attention on the boys' delinquency of the conflict variety. And it was this form of delinquency which led to major sanctions being imposed on them. The correlation is not complete but dividing sanctions into those which involve removal from home and those which do not, charges of assault occasioning actual bodily harm and assaulting the police, led to the former and more severe category of sanction. For instance case no. 1 had been sent to detention centre for assaulting a police officer, case no. 4 had been sent to Borstal for threatening behaviour and criminal damage, case no. 5 had been sent to Borstal for assault occasioning actual bodily harm and assaulting a police officer with intent to resist arrest and had been sent to prison for a further assault case, case no. 6 had been sent to Borstal as the result of four assault charges (two of which involved assaulting the police) and case no. 7 had been sent to Borstal on a charge of assaulting the police. The severity of the sanctions imposed on the boys for this form of activity rather than 'theft'-type activity is another highly significant reason for focusing attention on it and indicates the importance it had in the boys' lives.

THE BOYS AND THE COURT

The boys described in this study were familiar with the court-room setting. One of the things that impressed me when

I started 'hanging about' with them was that it was common practice for them to go into the public gallery of the local magistrates and crown courts and see 'what's going on'. And this was particularly the case when a person that the boys knew was on a charge. For instance, the Thursday night before a big court case on the Friday morning one of the boys told me: 'I'll go and pick up the dole and then go and see him put down – it'll fit in nicely.' The courtroom transaction with its description of deviant acts and its often long-term implications for those involved holds a particular fascination for many people and the boys were no exception. In addition to this general interest, the boys saw courtroom proceedings as an absorbing and inexpensive way of passing some of their free time. The courts were one of the few places where free entertainment was offered to them.

Most of the Luke Street boys had considerable experience of the courts whether as accused, witness or observer. All the boys referred to in this study as 'the boys on Casey's corner' went to court at least once during my time in the neighbourhood and some of them two or three times. If one of the boys went to court a group of the others would 'come along' and spend the morning in the public gallery. If it was a big case there would be as many as twenty of the boys in the gallery. For instance, the following is a description of Rappo's court case after a particularly intense week of contact with the courts. It should be remembered that the case took place on a weekday mid-morning, and that all the boys were, therefore, unemployed.

> Arrived at the court at ten o'clock and everybody seemed to be there. Went into magistrates court where Frankie and Pit were up on their charge of breaking a window at the youth club. Frankie pleaded not guilty and Pit pleaded guilty. The case was adjourned for a fortnight. Five of the West End boys were in the back of the court listening. Then we all including Pit and Frankie went into the back of the court to listen to Rappo's more serious case. He was up for Borstal training. There were now approximately twenty West End boys in the back of the court including Jacko (up tomorrow on theft charge).

The court cases themselves were also public knowledge in Luke Street itself. People in the area would know who was due to 'go up' and the results of court cases that had recently occurred. Like the actual events surrounding the incidents the court cases themselves became part of the 'conversation culture' of the area. Indeed I was continually surprised at the speed at which information about court cases was transmitted. For instance half an hour after the end of one of the cases in which the boys were involved I was back in Casey's and the result of the case had already been circulated around the bar. And the court cases themselves could occasionally produce major inter-personal and inter-family tensions in the area. Such a situation occurred during the court case concerning the 'rooftop' incident in which Mal was involved. Mal's family and Mal himself, as I have already noted, were not popular in the area and although many people observed the incident nobody was prepared to go to court as a witness. As Mal's father told me after the case:

> It's all the same with all of them down there. None of them will turn up when you're in court. And I tell you something else I shan't come down here again unless I can help it. If any of them want me to come down here and go witness I shan't do it. The lawyer tried to arrange it so that five witnesses would come down to court. The — s [another family in Luke Street] sent down a message saying 'we aren't interested, we didn't see nothing'.

THE INCIDENT GOES TO COURT

The way in which a charge resulting from incidents and neighbourhood events such as those described in this study was dealt with in the courts is of significance. When actually in the witness box the boys, like many other offenders, suffered from a lack of the formal articulacy necessary to describe their actions. They were thus unable to make their behaviour intelligible and therefore their actions were regarded in the stereotyped way as 'senseless' and 'meaningless'. They had no credibility and indicated a 'lack of integrity' and the 'wrong attitude'. This was particularly important for this group of boys because, as we have seen, their delinquent activity was not straightforward in the sense that larceny is straightforward. Typically they had been involved in conflict with the police and the boys had differing views as to what actually happened during these confrontations. And the boys were at the added disadvantage in the courts in that it was exactly this kind of confrontation and the more general aspects of vandalism that the people of Crossely found so disagreeable and difficult to understand.

In the courtroom the clash of the two worlds was in fact most apparent through the clash of the different meaning systems and different styles of speech. Although the boys attempted to 'get the story straight' amongst themselves before they went to court so that their versions of 'what happened' should not be inconsistent [2] they lacked the level of formal articulacy necessary to put forward 'reasons' for their activity. Phil Cohen has accurately described this difficulty in the following way:

> his [the delinquent's] non verbal behaviour is inserted into quite different communication contexts (court procedures, counselling by social worker, etc.) which function either to totally deprive it of its rationality (delinquency as madness) or else superimpose a totally false rationality (delinquency as badness). All this adds up to saying that working class kids are locked in a prison whose walls are invisible because they are made up of institutional processes.[3]

In reference to court cases involving alleged 'vandalism' or incidents the two most common sequences of exchange were as follows:

1. *Court Official* Why did you do this?
   Boy I don't know.
   Court Official Don't say you don't know. You must have had a reason. Nobody does anything without a reason.

2. *Boy* We didn't do that. I never touched him.

Police Prosecutor Are you calling the police officer a liar?

Boy Well, yes, we didn't do it.

Police Prosecutor That's a very serious business calling a police officer a liar. This man has got an excellent record of public service.

These composite sequences indicate the central problem that the boys faced when appearing in court on a typical charge. Their logic of why they were involved in these incidents wasn't accepted in court and they realised this. It was a question of their definition of 'what happened' in contrast to the police definition of 'what happened'. The boys, therefore, held basically the same view of the court system as they did of the police. Just as they believed that police methods were discriminatory so also did they believe that they rarely got a 'fair deal' in court. In their words it was 'rough justice'. The idea of fairness seemed almost irrelevant. As in every other system they had come into contact with, the boys believed that there were two distinct 'sides' – the winners and the losers. The winners were the judges, magistrates and other court personnel and the losers were 'the likes of us'.

One further point needs to be made about the boys' position in these courtroom transactions. Such transactions took place in a very public setting. For the majority of the cases the boys appeared with other members of the group or if they appeared as individuals there were likely to be other members of the group in the public gallery. Even if as individuals they had possessed the necessary formal articulacy to give an impression of remorse, because of the pressures of the public group context they were unlikely to do so. In court the individual boy had to maintain his personal integrity in the eyes of his fellows. For an individual to indicate that although the *group* was involved in delinquent activity, *he* was not or that his attitudes did not support such behaviour would have been highly problematic in terms of inter-group relations. The pressures of this public group setting were therefore very strong and along with the boys' lack of the necessary formal articulacy meant they apparently

offered no account for their activity and expressed no regret
at their actions. Although I can produce no evidence for
this I suggest that both of these factors played a part in
impressing upon the court the need to impose relatively
severe sanctions.

Because of their inability to articulate any defence for their
activity and the importance of not indicating too high a level
of regret or remorse for such activity, the boys' role in the
courtroom transactions was an essentially passive one. They
went to court, went into the dock, listened to the proceedings
with what could be referred to as hostile indifference and
waited for the bench to make its decision. They approached
the whole proceedings with a degree of fatalism and recognised the cumulative nature of court dispositions. If one
was sixteen and had already been fined, sent to attendance
centre and put on probation it was accepted that detention
centre or Borstal would be the next step. Anything less would
be a cause for celebration. One of the group for instance
was fined when he was convinced he was going to do three
months at a detention centre and the following evening
bought a round in Casey's – an unusual occurrence con-
sidering the boys' financial position. The boys did however
recognise that there were differences in the 'attitude' of
individual court officials. In particular clerks to the local
magistrates court were seen to wield major power and if
the boys were appearing in court with one of them – known
locally as Judge Jeffreys – it was anticipated that the court
disposition would be more severe than with the other. As
Mal told me after the rooftop incident: 'I was in —'s court.
That's why I only got fined. If I'd been in —'s I'd have been
sent down. No doubt about that.' Parker noted the same
beliefs in his Liverpool study: 'All officials will receive individual assessment if they seem to affect the prosecution
process. Thus the "judges" (magistrates) range from "At least
he listens to your side of the story" to "if you get her you've
had it, she enjoys sticking people down".'[4]

Allied to the generally fatalistic approach that the boys
adopted to the courtroom transactions they believed that they
were as a group 'unfairly' treated in the courts. It was believed
that a Luke Street address combined with membership of

one of the 'famous families' of the area (a local probation officer told me there was a group of families in the area who were 'entirely criminal in their history') was likely to prejudice their chances in court. I can produce no evidence to support this claim[5] although I do not believe it beyond the realms of possibility that the courts were so sensitised to the problematic nature of the area that they allocated more severe penalties to its residents in order to 'stamp out' the kind of behaviour that was seen to be associated with it. For instance throughout my time in the area there were repeated demands made in the local Press that the courts should deal severely with individuals involved in vandalism – a form of behaviour that as we have noted was publicly seen to be particularly associated with the West End. The actual policies and practices of the local courts are however beyond the scope of the present study. The important thing is that the boys believed they were dealt with in a discriminatory fashion because of their area of residence. This was also a belief that was held by adult members of the area as well:

Mrs P. They treat you differently in court if you come from around here. I can remember one time I was in court and I was having a bit of barney. Mr [clerk] told me 'Shut up – you aren't in Luke Street now'.

Mr T. You've got no chance if you come from around here. You can't get bail, you can't get legal aid. You can't get nothing.

The boys, and other members of the area, believed that they were unfairly 'picked upon' by the local courts and this again increased their feelings of isolation and of being special cases in the eyes of 'outsiders' and authority. And in this context it is interesting to note that the boys themselves made little distinction between the adult and the juvenile courts. Whether they were under or over seventeen they were simply 'going up'.

CONCLUSION

In this chapter on the outcome of court cases and the nature of the courtroom setting I have not attempted to deal exhaustively with the way in which individuals were processed through the local court system. It is however important to note that the courtroom transactions marked the final stage in the social production of delinquent behaviour in Luke Street. The courts formally registered individuals as either 'criminal' or 'delinquent' and in doing so played a significant role in two ways. First they produced a formal identity for the boys as being outside the law and this formal identity had implications for their future action. Secondly the court cases and the resultant heavy Press coverage increased the external image of Luke Street as a 'delinquent area' and this fed back into the circular system the anticipations and expectations which could lead to further trouble.

10

HOUSING POLICY AND THE ORGANISATION OF POSSIBILITY

It's the place that does it. It's the area that changes people.

Mrs P.

The challenge of sociology remains as it was expressed by C. Wright Mills – to understand how wider social arrangements affect the lives of individuals. In this book I have attempted to go beyond a description of the illegal act and the immediate contexts in which it occurs. I have attempted to recognise the conflict, imagery and disharmony of our urban society and to see how such conflict, imagery and disharmony is organised so that at the everyday and local level delinquency becomes a possibility.

The starting point then of the study is the social construction of Luke Street – its physical characteristics, the people who were allocated accommodation there and the meanings that came to be associated with it. Luke Street originated from a process of residential selection which can relegate some areas to the bottom of a hierarchy of desirability: the families who are least able to compete in the struggle for 'better' accommodation in the private or public sector, end up living there. It was not a question of 'like attracting like' but more directly one of economic power and policy decisions. And out of this original process of selection grew secondary processes. One of the most important of these was the way that the neighbourhood came to be regarded by outsiders. It is the contention of this study that because of the barriers to communication between Luke Street and the wider community the two worlds grew further apart and beliefs and definitions came to play a correspondingly more important part and had significant behavioural consequences.

The families which were sent to live in Luke Street in the 1950s and 1960s faced problems which resulted from their position in the wider economic and social structures in which they found themselves. A significant proportion of the heads of the families sent to Luke Street were unemployed and from the details presented in Chapter 2 it is obvious that many of the others faced all the difficulties that surrounded and continue to surround the large family whose head is unskilled and must rely on employment which is insecure. As an extension of this I argue that these difficulties were one of the prime reasons that their 'standards' were regarded as unsatisfactory by the various housing department personnel who had visited them and allocated them accommodation in the West End. The grouping together of these families produced a situation whose two key characteristics were the increased visibility of the difficulties faced by the individual families and the group as a whole, and the growing up together of the children of the large families leading to an 'adolescent boom'. These two factors superimposed onto the other more general disadvantages that young people in such areas face of limited educational, recreational and employment opportunities had produced a situation by the mid-1960s in which the likelihood of delinquent activity and police – adolescent contact was amplified by the joint processes of the developing external stereotype of the neighbourhood in terms of lawless youth and the development inside the neighbourhood of a tradition of adolescent 'wildness'. And these processes had continued until by the late 1960s the behaviour of the young people in the neighbourhood was seen externally as anti-social and the boys of the neighbourhood increasingly saw themselves as being 'outside the law'. The boys associated the neighbourhood with 'trouble' and just as they were sensitive to the possibility of such trouble so also were the representatives of external authority equally sensitive. And increasing the importance of this mutual expectation was the fact that one of the few available avenues of identity construction for the boys was in terms of their relationship with authority. In this process of identity construction 'trouble' and the meanings attached to it were of central importance.

These pressures and processes can be illustrated by the following historical model of the relationship between the creation of Luke Street and 'trouble' in the neighbourhood. This sequence should be seen in the same way as, and inter-related with, the sequence in Chapter 2 which described the general 'decline' of Luke Street. And although this sequence relates specifically to delinquency of a conflict nature, in which the boys were particularly involved, it has implications for delinquency of a more material nature in the area.

(i) Luke Street in the 1950s relatively 'quiet' in terms of adolescent 'trouble'. Large families of original tenants grown up and left and so a degree of under-occupation of homes in the neighbourhood.

(ii) From late 1950s onwards arrival in Luke Street of very large families. Therefore, disproportionate number of young children in the neighbourhood.

(iii) These families already facing difficulties in achieving required 'standards' in 'coping' and in 'making ends meet'.

(iv) Children growing up in a *public* setting because of over-crowding in the home, lack of organised recreational facilities in the neighbourhood.

(v) *Public* nature of lives of young people in neighbour-hood leads to beginning of small-scale local vandalism and 'trouble' on the streets.

(vi) Effects of this exacerbated for older groups by high level of adolescent unemployment.

(vii) Because of this a 'tradition' of contact with the police grows up in the neighbourhood.

(viii) External stereotype or 'reputation' of area developed by mid-1960s and begins to have amplifying effect on difficulties faced by young people in the neigh-bourhood.

(ix) Self-perpetuating process of increase in number of incidents and 'trouble'.

(x) Stereotyping as 'lawless' leads to more police sur-veillance and increased police attention to certain

forms of public behaviour on the part of young
people in the area.

To understand the position of the group of boys who used
to hang about on Casey's corner in 1971–3 they must be
seen as one group in a chain of such groups. Their difficulties
were the end product of the various interconnected processes
which affected their neighbourhood. They were the victims
of a circular process initiated by the physical characteristics
and composition of their neighbourhood and through which
they had come to be seen and to see themselves as 'wild'.
Indeed taken to its logical conclusion the argument is that
we can only understand the position of the boys if we go
back forty years to the decision of the local planners to
create a disproportionate number of large houses and flats
in that part of the West End of Crossley.

   Of course there is no way to show beyond argument that
the boys' difficulties were intimately linked with the processes
of neighbourhood construction which affected Luke Street.
Nor indeed can it be 'proved' that their difficulties were
inextricably linked with the extreme stereotypes that outsiders
had of the West End. No methods exist, or will exist, to
illustrate those connections conclusively. And yet the
evidence concerning the development of Luke Street would
suggest that such indeed was the case and that the disadvantages of the boys can be most fruitfully examined from this
standpoint. The combination of these various processes, in
particular the fact that Luke Street had sunk to the bottom
of the housing hierarchy and the stereotype of 'trouble' that
surrounded it were accurately summed up to me by a twenty-
year-old West Ender:

> Say you're in [neighbouring area] and they ask you where
> you're from and you say the West End. They say are you
> one of the hard nuts then. Once you've got labelled from
> around here that's it. There might be a few bad ones but
> they're not all bad . . . They say they play tig with choppers
> round here . . . If you say you come from around here
> they say fancy living there. I wouldn't live there rent free.
> But most of them who say that were born and brought
> up around here.[1]

There was an activation of the mythology on both sides, and in this the perceived characteristics of the area played a central part. The police believed that the 'hard core' section of the West End was troublesome and the boys believed that 'it's really wild around here'. Indeed it was not by chance that some of the boys talked of leaving the West End as synonymous with 'keeping out of trouble'. There was thus collusion between the boys and the police about the characteristics of the neighbourhood and this collusion played its part in the genesis of conflict. Increasing the effect of this process was the fact that because of their structural position an identity 'outside the law' was one of the few that was readily available to the boys. In terms of action on the street this had the amplificatory effect of their having to create audiences where none previously existed. And in this they shared a degree of insight in terms of the mechanics of individual incidents and stressed the intensity of the conflict. Their position *vis-à-vis* the control agencies increasingly became one of the central elements of their self-identity. With other channels of identity construction blocked to them the boys therefore sought contact with the police in order to develop a meaning for their lives. They flirted with the police and the police were ready suitors.

SOME NOTES ON POLICY IMPLICATIONS

The individually orientated 'social work' approach which is basic to our orientation to adolescent delinquency is virtually useless in dealing with a situation such as prevails in Luke Street. Indeed it may well be counter-productive. Imagine for instance what the social worker is likely to do with one of the Luke Street boys on supervision. His primary orientation is likely to be the family. Family relationships will be discussed, attitudes will be explored and the social worker will operate as a 'warm supportive adult'.[2] Contact between the social worker and the boy will take place in the office – in the case of Crossley a large modern block nearly two miles away from Luke Street – or at best in the family home. And that contact will take place during office hours. But delinquency of the kind described in this study occurs in the evening and on the corner and individualised methods of social work intervention have no way of dealing with the processes that lead to it. Indeed, it can be argued that the main reason why there was no change in Luke Street was that the outside professional workers only operated at the level of individual problems. Although many of them had a vague belief that if the community could function at a more 'meaningful' level the problems of the neighbourhood would somehow magically disappear, the difficulties which were intimately linked with the processes affecting the residential group as a whole, were individualised and thus discounted.

The answer to the problems of Luke Street does not lie therefore in the kind of social work with which we are familiar in relation to delinquency. It is necessary to change our emphasis from the individual and to counteract the processes that are involved in the creation of the delinquent area.

The most obvious approach, but one which is difficult to put into operation, is to foster the kind of sensitivity in planning and allocation policies whereby the development of other 'West Ends' in fifteen or twenty years' time could be prevented, and there would be less call for the services of future generations of trouble workers.

It was local planning and housing department policies that produced Luke Street. The action of the police and the stereotyping of Luke Street as a 'bad' area were crucial but secondary processes. The first implication of the present study is therefore to stress the dangers of a high level of child density. Each local authority has its own housing stock which produces its own set of difficulties. But in Crossley a more sensitive allocation procedure in the 1950s and 1960s would have avoided the eventual characteristics of the West End. There are other parts of the West End which in terms of physical amenities were not so very different from Luke Street and in which particular houses could have been, if necessary, converted to accommodate large families. Thus if a housing department happens to suffer from a planning legacy of a particular area with a disproportionate amount of large accommodation in it then it is necessary to accept that in the interests of the area as a whole a degree of under-occupation is necessary.

In terms of the more general problem of allocating particular families to particular areas the majority of writers[3] have concluded that within the context of a competitive housing market the 'bad' area created by allocation policies is inevitable. And some commentators have also seen allocation decisions of the housing departments as being roughly in tune with the wishes of the different groups of residents themselves. This may possibly be true in particular areas but I regard it with a high degree of scepticism. Certainly the policies of local housing departments nicely coincide with the demands of their more economically advantaged tenants. But I have seen very little evidence of policies coinciding with the wishes of disadvantaged families or groups of tenants. The nice property goes to the nice tenants (niceness being defined in terms of clear rent books, high standards of furnishings, etc.). Thus the 'respectable' families may certainly wish to group themselves together but I do not accept that those classified as being of 'low' standard constantly seek out others who are facing similar difficulties. The suggestion comes dangerously close to a belief that 'they choose to be like that' and that their problems are of their own choosing.

It is essential to recognise that in following community typifications of who the 'good' tenant is, local allocation policies exacerbate the problems of those tenants who are regarded as less satisfactory. A necessary corollary of giving good property to 'good' tenants is giving bad property to 'bad' tenants. And in adopting this policy many local housing departments have forced specific areas into a dramatic decline.

Local authority housing departments have a very definite responsibility not to adopt the apparently extreme and rigid policies that produced in the post-war years the situation in the West End of Crossley where streets and blocks of flats were categorised as suitable only for the 'worst type of applicant'. The process of self-selection on the part of the 'better' applicants does lead to a lack of choice for those who are categorised as the 'least desirable' and yet at the same time the local housing departments are in a position to regulate the rigid and extreme dichotomy between housing areas and thus avoid for individual neighbourhoods the headlong spiral into decline.

A FINAL NOTE OF PESSIMISM

Sensitive allocation procedures have their uses. But in the end they are partially neutralised by the more basic arrangements of power in society. *Techniques* of social intervention are not enough to counteract the creation of the delinquent area. The economic disadvantages of those families that are forced to move to the least desirable areas will not be changed by piecemeal local tinkering, nor will the drastically severe employment difficulties of young school-leavers such as the Luke Street boys be affected in this way. Indeed the increased rationalisation of urban life and work may mean that in the future there are more rather than less Luke Streets.

Like it or not when we are trying to understand what happens on Casey's corner we are forced back into wide-scale issues of housing, employment and the distribution of social power. As Townsend has recently stated: 'just as some areas are declining, others are experiencing boom. The decline or deprivation of some areas is not explicable except in relation to the advance of the affluence of other – whether regionally or nationally. The conditions within each type of area have to be related to some standard, or alternatively to other parts of the economy or the social structure as distributed spatially.[4] The connections have been made for a long time. Now more than ever with the creation of a new class – the welfare and social work recipients – and the creation of ideologies to maintain them in their disadvantaged position, we must make these connections.

APPENDIX:

SOME ISSUES OF RESEARCH METHODOLOGY

In this study I have used different categories of data. To describe the development of Luke Street and the difficulties of the boys I have utilised housing department records, official police statistics, Press reports of delinquent behaviour and interview material from individuals who in various work roles had been in contact with the area. But a substantial proportion of the study is based on data collected actually during my contact with the residents of Luke Street and it is this aspect of my research approach – participant observation – which I wish to discuss in this appendix.

The adoption of the participant – observation approach is particularly appropriate to the study of delinquent behaviour. Recent theoretical formulations of the nature of delinquent activity have stressed four aspects of such activity: (i) the situationally based *subjective definitions* of the individual or group concerning delinquent activity; (ii) the specific local *opportunity structure* with which particular groups of adolescents are faced; (iii) the *processes* whereby delinquent acts are committed; and (iv) the *interactions* between the definers and the defined. If this is a fact a productive approach to the analysis of delinquent behaviour then it is immediately apparent that participant observation is an appropriate method of investigation. Indeed it is perhaps the *most* appropriate method of research into delinquency. The traditional method of interviewing delinquents abstracted from the actual time – place location of delinquency may offe interesting general information but can offer little in terms of an understanding of the *process* of delinquency.

PARTICIPANT OBSERVATION IN LUKE STREET

The full-time fieldwork for this study took just over eighteen
months. Over and above this I maintained contact with the
area and some of the boys for a further two years. I started
my contact with the area in late 1971 and initially worked
as an assistant in a local youth club. This club although
more than half a mile away from Luke Street had the only
indoor football pitch in the area and people travelled from
quite a distance to use it. Although most of them did not
use the other meagre facilities that the club had to offer
a fair number of the Luke Street boys regularly turned up
to play football there. And it was in breaks from my role
as a referee that I began developing contact with them. At
this stage I made a few tentative remarks that I would like
to hang around with them and see what life was like in
Luke Street but these were met with disinterest. My fieldnotes
for that period indicate the reaction that these initial advances
met with:

> Tonight I was talking to Rappo and as casually as possible
> I suggested that I would like to come down to Luke Street
> and hang about with them and see 'what the score is'. He
> looked at me in a rather pitying way, shrugged his
> shoulders and returned to the subject of football.

But after a couple of months working at the club I was invited to come back after the game for a drink with them at
Casey's. This offer I gratefully received and thereafter I was a
regular visitor to Casey's and the scene of my operations
changed.

The first evening I was in Casey's I was lucky enough
to get into conversation with Jimmy, who as I have already
noted was later to become a good friend. I saw him fairly
regularly after that first meeting and he seemed to take considerable pleasure in talking about the area. At one stage
he was in the habit of introducing me to people 'who might
be interesting' and I well remember one evening when
Jimmy and I sat down at a side table in Casey's and he
produced a pencil and paper and, as if he had been trained
in the skills of sociometry, began to draw a detailed diagram

of the contact patterns amongst the people at the bar. I was lucky to find such an able research assistant and some of the ideas and information that I have used in this study about life in Luke Street must be attributed to him.

My contact with the local boys actually on their home territory was not so immediately favourable. Although it was entirely acceptable for me to drink at the bar with other men of my own age it was not initially accepted for me to stand outside the pub door on the corner where the boys congregated. People of my age in Luke Street had 'left the corner' some five or ten years previously. After several months during which time I suspect I was suffering from more anomie than any of the boys I eventually defined for myself a role as something of an expert on legal matters in general and the local court system in particular. In this role I was able to initiate contact through advising the boys. Such reciprocal relationships are in fact essential for the development of fieldwork contact in a situation such as this. The pure observer role is impossible to maintain.

This reciprocal relationship developed in the following months and it gradually became acceptable that I should hang about with the boys. After all if I was to help them in the court situation it was essential that I should know 'what the score is'. By the end of the first six months my interactions with the boys were becoming increasingly easy and it was accepted that I should not only hang about with them on the corner but go to their homes, pubs, cafes, dance halls, the courts, employment offices and on general excursions outside the neighbourhood with them. On the basis of my initial 'expertise' in legal matters I had developed a role very similar to that described by Liebow in his study of unemployed men in Washington: 'On several different counts I was an outsider but I was also a participant in the full sense of the word. The people I was observing knew that I was observing them, yet they allowed me to participate in their activities and take part in their lives to a degree that continues to surprise me. Some "exploited" me not as an outsider but rather as one who, as a rule, had more resources than they did.'[1]

My role in Luke Street cannot therefore be seen entirely

within the framework of participant observation as it is typically defined. I *did* offer the boys legal advice and I *did* conduct some relatively structured discussion groups. But I do believe that where it was most important – hanging about on the street and the corner and witnessing the incidents – I was relatively well accepted and my presence did not in fact impede or alter the normal forms of social interaction in this context. In fact on a number of occasions as is indicated in earlier chapters I was regarded by outsiders as being an older member of the group. For instance on one occasion I was standing in Luke Street with three of the boys and a police car pulled up beside us. We got into a conversation with the driver and one of our group asked him what made him join the police. He looked at us, me included, for several moments and then remarked: 'Well if you're thick you either go in the police like me or you end up on the street like you.'

The *technique* of participant observation was therefore, I suggest, appropriate for understanding the position of the boys and the subjective meanings associated with it. But research into behaviour regarded as problematic produces distinct problems the solution of which depends on the particular research worker and the particular situation. First, if his study is to be at all effective, he will sooner or later be asked to witness or to be involved in legally prohibited behaviour. As Polsky notes: 'if one is to effectively study adult criminals in their natural setting, he must make the moral decision that in some ways he will break the law himself. He need not be a "participant observer" and commit the criminal acts being studied, yet he has to witness such acts or be taken into confidence about them and not blow the whistle.'[2] In fact not only did I witness illegal behaviour and fail to carry out my duty as a citizen and report it but I was also requested to be directly involved in such behaviour. The boys were in fact quite perceptive about the particular pressures the field researcher is under: for instance before one of the visits to the docks late at night Frankie told me 'you know you'll have to come with us – the lads won't think the same of you if you don't'. On this general issue I agree with Polsky that one has to take the decision of whether or not to be included in illegal behaviour on the basis of the particular characteristics of the research context, the particular character of the relationship developed with the 'subjects' and the relative value to the study of being involved in such behaviour.[3] But the decision is a difficult one and the neophyte researcher would be well advised to be familiar with the story, possibly apocryphal, of the French criminologist who was researching a criminal gang but became so involved that he was given a prison sentence and had to change the area of his research to social interaction in the prison setting.[4]

Related to this is the more important problem of one's influence on individuals involved in delinquency. This involves the general problem of being a nonentity – the traditional fly-on-the-wall role – and operating to change if only in a small way the situation one is involved in. And it is this particular problem which is most apparent in research of the kind described in this study, which is dealing with *young* people involved in *problematic* behaviour. I am well aware of the argument put forward by Polsky and others that:

> Field study of adult criminals requires among other things giving up, indeed carefully avoiding, any and every kind of social-work orientation (such as a concern to 're-habilitate' criminals); but in sociology's struggle to become a science it has been precisely criminology . . . that has been least successful in freeing itself from traditional social work concerns.[5]

I hope that I never set out to 'rehabilitate' anybody in Luke Street but at the same time because of the perspectives one develops one perhaps has a responsibility in terms of the people one is working with. Take for example the question of delinquent incidents with which two of the chapters in this study are specifically concerned. I have argued that (i) these incidents involved a natural progression of moves and counter-moves and (ii) that this progression was discernible to the observer. Should the researcher let these processes develop into a final confrontation and possibly an incident and then lean back and say 'I told you so – my theory's correct' or should he use the perspective he has developed about the timing, location and development of incidents to 'defuse' the situation? I can give no firm guidelines on this problem but suggest that this is a tension of which the researcher should be aware before engaging in this kind of research. And in my own case I would hope that by the end of my research I had reached a position in which I was beginning to discard the role of pure observer and becoming involved, if only in a small way, with trying to effect some changes not in the boys themselves, but in the structures and contexts in which they operated.

There is the more general, and again essentially ethical problem, of the effects of criminological research on the subject group. If, as is argued in this study, the boys' behaviour was amplified by the external stereotypes of it, what is the effect of someone coming in to study it? Obviously one only studies things which are worth studying but what implications does this carry for the subjects themselves? Yablonsky has argued that a non-moralising interest in delinquency, such as was later to be advocated by David Matza, constitutes a romantic encouragement of the criminal.[6] And the basic ethical issue is stated by Erikson in the following way: 'so long as we suggest that a method we use has at least some potential for harming others, we are in the extremely awkward position of having to weigh the scientific and social benefits of that procedure against its possible costs in human discomfort'.[7] My own feelings are that this tension can never be entirely satisfactorily resolved but that the researcher does have a responsibility to be constantly sensitive about the effects of his presence on the subjects he is working with and not to be involved in activity which he believes *increases* the likelihood of their being involved in behaviour defined as problematic. In practical terms this may well necessitate him minimising his own importance as perceived by the group. The accepted nonentity may well in this sense be a more ethically appropriate role than that of the respected investigator.

Finally it is worth noting that one also has a responsibility for the form of one's research report if that report or sections of it are to be published. Although it is necessary to concentrate on deviant behaviour in terms of analysis, it is important to paint a picture which encompasses the normality, dignity and integrity of the people one has made one's subjects.

The sociologist's responsibility to his subjects is therefore a continuous one and does not stop once he returns to the sheltered employment of the university to write about his findings. In planning a study, in conducting it and in writing it the sociologist should have his subjects looking over his shoulder. He has a responsibility neither consciously nor unconsciously to contribute to the stereotypes which afflict relatively powerless groups in society.

NOTES AND REFERENCES

CHAPTER 1

1. See the introductory essay in A. E. Bottoms and J. Baldwin, *The Urban Criminal* (Tavistock, 1976).
2. The best account of Chicago sociology remains T. P. Morris, *The Criminal Area. A study in social ecology* (Routledge & Kegan Paul, 1957).
3. R. E. Park, *Human Communities: The collected papers of R. E. Park* (Free Press, 1952) p. 16.
4. H. Mannheim, *Juvenile Delinquency in an English Middletown* (Kegan Paul, Trench Trubner and Co. Ltd, 1948).
5. H. Mannheim, ibid., p. 32.
6. T. Ferguson, *The Young Delinquent in his Social Setting* (Oxford University Press, 1952).
7. T. Ferguson, ibid., p. 17.
8. T. P. Morris, op. cit., 1957.
9. H. Jones, 'Approaches to an Ecological Study', *British Journal of Delinquency*, vol. 8, no. 4 (1958) pp. 277–93.
10. J. Spencer, *Stress and Release on an Urban Estate* (Tavistock, 1964).
11. C. P. Wallis and R. Maliphant, 'Delinquent Areas in the County of London: Ecological Factors', *British Journal of Criminology*, vol. 7, no. 3 (1967) pp. 250–84.
12. C. P. Wallis and R. Maliphant, ibid., p. 259.
13. J. Baldwin and A. E. Bottoms, op. cit., 1976.
14. L. Taylor, *Deviance and Society* (Michael Joseph, 1971) p. 131.
15. J. Rex and R. Moore, *Race, Community and Conflict: a study of Sparkbrook* (Oxford University Press, 1967).
16. J. Rex and R. Moore, ibid., p. 273.
17. J. Rex and R. Moore, ibid., p. 276.
18. The 1969 C.H.A.C. report noted that 'some housing authorities took up a moralistic attitude towards applicants; the underlying philosophy seemed to be that council tenancies were to be given only to those who "deserved" them and that the "most deserving" were to get the best houses.' Central Housing

Advisory Council Report, *Council Housing: Purposes, Procedures and Priorities* (H.M.S.O., 1969) para. 96.

19. See for example R. Bordessa, 'Perception of social environment and residential desires. A South Liverpool view of the city and Merseyside', Unpublished Ph.D. thesis (University of Liverpool, 1971).

20. This issue is now of course complicated by the introduction of rent and rate rebates, although these were not available during the period with which this study is concerned in respect to the creation of Luke Street.

21. See S. Damer and R. Madigan, 'The Housing Investigator' *New Society* (25 July 1974) pp. 226 – 7.

22. V. Walters, 'Dreadful Enclosures: Detoxifying an Urban Myth', unpublished paper presented to conference on cognitive and emotional Aspects of Urban Life New York City (June 1972).

23. E. Lemert, *Social Pathology* (McGraw-Hill, 1951) p. 55.

24. The serious student might however look at N. Goldman, 'The Differential Selection of Offenders for Court Appearance' (National Council on Crime and Delinquency, 1963); G. W. O'Connor and N. A. Watson, 'Juvenile Delinquency and Youth Crime: the Police Role' (Washington International Association of Chiefs of Police, 1964); I. Piliavin and S. Briar, 'Police Encounters with Juveniles' in *Deviance: the Interactionist Perspective*, ed. E. Rubington and M. S. Weinberg (Collier-Macmillan, 1968) pp. 137 – 45; C. Werthman and I, Piliavin, 'Gang Members and the Police', in *The Police*, ed. D. J. Bordua (John Wiley, 1967'; W. F. Hohenstein, 'Factors Influencing the Police Disposition of Juvenile Offenders', in *Delinquency: Selected Studies*, ed. T.Sellin and M. E. Wolfgang (John Wiley, 1969' pp. 138 – 49; T. N. Ferdinand and E. G. Luchterhand, 'Inner City Youth, the Police, the Juvenile Court and Justice', *Social Problems*, vol. 17 (1969 – 70) pp. 510 – 27; D. J. Black and A. J. Reiss, 'Police Control of Juveniles', *American Sociological Review*, vol. 25 (1970) pp. 63 – 77; C. Werthman and I. Piliavin, 'Gang Members and Ecological Conflict', in *Juvenile Delinquency: a Book of Readings*, 2nd ed., ed. R. Giallombardo (John Wiley, 1972) pp. 291 – 314. Those with less time to spare might look at the excellent review of this body of research in S. Box, *Deviance, Reality and Society* (Holt, Rinehart and Winston, 1971).

25. A. Cicourel, *The Social Organization of Juvenile Justice* (John Wiley, 1968) p. 328.

26. D. Chapman, *Sociology and the Stereotype of the Criminal* (Tavistock, 1968).

27. See A. L. Stinchcombe, 'Institutions of Privacy in the Determination of Police Administrative Practice', *American Journal of Sociology*, vol. LXIX, no. 2 (1963) p. 150. Stinchcombe argues that the effects of privacy are to reduce the liability of those who possess it to legal scrutiny.

28. D. Chapman, op. cit., p. 11.

29. J. Lambert, *Crime, Police and Race Relations* (Oxford University Press, 1970).

30. J. Lambert, ibid., p. 164.

31. M. Cain, *Society and the Policeman's Role* (Routledge & Kegan Paul, 1973).

32. See G. Armstrong and M. Wilson, 'Social Problems, Social Control and the Case of Easterhouse', paper presented to B.S.A. Conference (1971). See also G. Armstrong and M. Wilson, City Politics and Deviancy Amplification' in *Politics and Deviance* eds. I. Taylor and L. Taylor (Penguin, 1973) pp. 61– 89.

33. G. Armstrong and M. Wilson ibid. (1973) p. 83.

CHAPTER 2

1. N. Dennis, 'The Popularity of the neighbourhood Community Idea' *Readings in Urban Sociology*, in ed. R. E. Pahl (Pergamon Press, 1968) p. 75.

2. I was given access to the housing department folders on each of the sixty nine households.

3. Damer in his Glasgow Study noted 'when slum clearance got going in a big way in Glasgow in the 1930s it was the firm intention of the corporation to judge tenants' worthiness for a council house, and to sort out the "inefficient," "indifferent" and the simply "dirty" tenants and to train them in domestic science. This breed of what has been called "municipal socialism" involved the selection of tenants according to various criteria of worthiness. These criteria are contained in a form which housing visitors used on an inspection visit of potential tenants' houses; besides listing tenants' address essential demographic data, and whether or not their rent was paid up the form used in the 1930s said:

Type of people	Good/fair/needs supervision/unsuitable
Cleanliness	Good/medium/poor
Furniture	Good/medium/poor/none.'

S. Damer, 'The Sociology of a Dreadful Enclosure,' *The Sociological Review*, vol. 22, no. 2 (May 1974).

4. Some comments by housing officials indicated that they worked on an A, B, C, D, categorisation of the desirability of tenants.
5. There is no evidence to suggest as did the housing committee report that this was also a pre-war policy.
6. This rapid changeover can be seen as a form of the 'tipping' which has been described in the literature on housing and racial minorities. A study of Chicago found no instance between 1940 and 1952 of a mixed neighbourhood (a neighbourhood with 25 per cent-plus of blacks) in which succession from white to black occupancy was arrested. It was found that succession rarely reversed once the black population had reached 10 per cent. O. Dudley and B. Duncan, *The Negro Population of Chicago* (University of Chicago Press, 1957).
7. Some of the letters written by Luke Street residents to the housing department indicated that they had heard of vacant corporation property and then applied specifically for it. An example of this was the Luke Street lady who walked around the new estates and took a note of vacant property and then wrote to the housing department to see if there was a possibility of transfer.
8. David A. Kirby, 'The Inter-war Council Dwelling', *Town Planning Review*, vol. 42, no. 3 (July 1971) p. 251.
9. S. Damer, 'The Sociology of a Reputation', unpublished paper presented to British Sociological Association Conference (Sept 1972) p. 1.

CHAPTER 3

1. The Home Office refused direct access to the records and they were collected by a member of the local criminal records office.
2. As in the previous chapter I am including in this section details of the last families to live in the now vacant property in Luke Street.
3. This figure of seventy-eight includes two individuals other than members of the nuclear families hence the discrepancy between the earlier number of family offenders.
4. Because of the importance of this pattern I checked with the criminal records officer who assured me that all of an individual's offences, whether in the 1930s or the 1970s, would be recorded on their files.
5. For instance R. A. Cloward and L. Ohlin, *Delinquency and Opportunity* (Routledge and Kegan Paul, 1961).

CHAPTER 4

1. S. Cohen, *Folk Devils and Moral Panics* (MacGibbon and Kee, 1972) p. 40.
2. For a general discussion see K. Lynch, *The Image of the City* (M.I.T. Press, 1960).
3. G. D. Suttles, *The Social Order of the Slum* (University of Chicago Press, 1968) p. 25.
4. G. D. Suttles, *The Social Construction of Communities* (University of Chicago Press, 1972).
5. G. D. Suttles, ibid., p. 239.
6. E. V. Walters, op. cit., 1972.
7. See P. Collision, *The Cutteslowe Walls. A Study in Social Class* (Faber, 1963).
8. By far the best British analysis of the production and characteristics of a neighbourhood reputation is the work of Damer on the Broomloan Road estate in Govan which came to be known as 'Wine Alley'. See S. Damer, op. cit. (1974) pp. 221–48.
9. S. Hall, 'A World at one with Itself' in *The Manufacture of News*, ed. S. Cohen and J. Young (Constable, 1973) p. 86.
10. H. Cox and D. Morgan, *City Politics and the Press* (Cambridge University Press, 1973) p. 108.
11. The *Crossley News* reported many bizarre attempts to cut down vandalism. One of these was the suggestion that the new lavatories in an adjoining area should be built outside the town clerk's office window so he could keep an eye on them.
12. All of the Press reports in this chapter were published during the research period.
13. Casey's, see Chapter 8.
14. See S. Cohen, 'Campaigning against Vandalism' in *Vandalism*, ed. C. Ward (Architectural Press, 1973) pp. 215–58.
15. S. Cohen in C. Ward (ed.). ibid. (1973) pp. 321–8.
16. H. J. Gans, *The Urban Villagers* (Free Press, 1962).
17. J. Martin and J. Fitzpatrick, op. cit. (1965) p. 96. See also R. Weiner, 'Twentieth Century Middle Class Colonizers', *Social Work Today*, vol. 4, no. 2 (19 April 1973).
18. There were also the more individual indicators of the way in which the wider community felt about the area. For instance as the mother who had the five-foot sign saying 'OUT OF ORDER DUE TO VANDALISM' immediately outside her front door told me, 'no wonder people think badly of us if they put signs like that up'.
19. Suttles has noted 'how nearly the Addams are resembles a

prison community or any other population that is not initially credited with a capacity to behave in an approved social manner'. G. Suttles, op. cit. (1968) p. 27.

CHAPTER 5

1. For details of the research methodology see Appendix.
2. After I had finished spending time regularly in Luke Street, I told that somebody in the neighbourhood had described me as a 'gobshit'. This offended me at first. The I realised that social researchers are the ultimate 'gobshits' as their words are rarely backed up by action.
3. This kind of humour had its counterpart in the case of the professionals who came into contact with Luke Street. The humour of 'that's the kind of thing you expect to happen down there' was often an integral aspect of the way in which they talked about the neighbourhood. For instance before I got to know the area I was told by a local priest, 'they play a lot of tennis down in Luke Street – they throw the rubbish backwards and forwards over the garden fences'.
4. E. W. Burgess in E. W. Burgess and D. J. Bordua (eds), *Contributions to Urban Sociology* (Univ. of Chicago Press, 1964) p. 596.
5. C. Valentine, *Culture and Poverty: Critique and Counter Proposals* (Univ. of Chicago Press, 1968) p. 15.
   Birmingham Centre for Contemporary Cultural Studies, 1972)

CHAPTER 6

1. Throughout this and the following chapters I have used pseudonyms for each of the boys.
2. See Appendix for a more detailed account of the research methodology.
3. The ages given for the boys are for early 1973 – the end of the research period.
4. R. A. Cloward and L. Ohlin, op. cit. (1961).
5. The actual income of the boys is, therefore, in sharp contradiction to what could be called the 'affluent youth theory' of delinquent activity – the idea that boys such as these lack any form of internal discipline because they've had everything handed to them on a plate.
6. J. Patrick, *A Glasgow Gang Observed* (Eyre Methuen, 1973).
7. P. Cohen, 'Subcultural Conflict and Working Class Community', *Working Papers in Cultural Studies* (University of

Birmingham Centre for Contemporary Cultural Studies, 1972 p. 49.

8. The activities of the I.R.A. particularly with reference to their designation of 'no go' areas was a talking point amongst the boys. Jokes were made about Luke Street being a 'no go' area. Casey's also had a large painted 'BOGSIDE INN' and 'I.R.A.' on one of its walls for some of my time in the neighbourhood.

9. E. Liebow, *Tally's Corner: Washington D.C.* (Routledge and Kegan Paul, 1967) p. 136.

CHAPTER 7

1. An exception is in Brian Jackson's, *Working Class Community*, (Pelican Books, 1972) see ch. 7 'Riot'. Also see the descriptions of 'delinquency on the move' in H. Parker, *The View from the Boys* (David and Charles, 1974).

2. S. Cohen, 'Directions for Research an Adolescent Group Violence and Vandalism', *British Journal of Criminology*, vol. 97, no. 4 (1971) p. 333.

3. S. Cohen, ibid., p. 334.

4. S. Cohen, ibid., p. 334.

5. D. Matza, *Delinquency and Drift* (John Wiley, 1964) p. 102.

6. The various problems faced in carrying out research into aspects of neighbourhood life and more specifically into the dynamics of conflict can offer useful insights for an analysis of the phenomena themselves. This is particularly the case in the observation and description of incidents where there is the difficulty of being in the right location at the right time. But the solution of this research problem indicates one of the key characteristics of the nature of incidents. Because of the way in which incidents build up, the way in which they are anticipated and in some cases the way in which they have 'traditional' aspects it is relatively easy to be prepared for their occurrence. The main incidents or sequences of events described in this chapter were to a greater or lesser degree anticipated in that the circumstances were recognised as having the potential for conflict. Thus simply 'hanging around' and developing a sensitivity to the process involved in the build-up to the incident can lead to being in the right location at the right time.

7. The researcher in a situation such as this soon learns, however, not to ask too many questions. To be constantly enquiring as to why people do things that are defined as deviant can

easily imply that he himself regards their behaviour in the stereotyped way as being 'senseless'. Indeed a retrospective analysis of the kinds of questions the researcher feels an idiot asking can tell him a good deal about the situations he has been in.

8. C. Wright Mills, 'Situated Actions and Vocabularies of Motive', *American Sociological Review*, v (1940) pp. 904–13. On the nature of 'accounts' see also M. B. Scott and S. M. Lyman, 'Accounts', *American Sociological Review* xxxiii (1968) pp. 46–62. Also L. Taylor, 'The significance and Interpretation of Replies to Motivational Questions: The Case of Sex Offenders', *Sociology*, vol. 6, no. 1 (Jan. 1972) pp. 23–40. Also several studies have implied that 'motives' for deviant behaviour are in some cases learnt after the event. See for example J. Auld, 'Drug Use: The Mystification of Accounts' in *Contemporary Social Problems in Britain*, eds. R. V. Bailey and J. Young (Saxon House, 1973) pp. 145–69.

9. Police patrol car – because of the wide red stripes on the side.

10. This clustering is interpreted in different ways by different people. For instance, the local youth leader quoted in the previous chapter told me 'It's a sort of boredom. They go so long before they've got to blow up. Then they go quiet for a few more months.'

11. The walls of Casey's acted as a tabloid for events in the neighbourhood. Another message at this time read 'COPPERS WATCH OUT ON BOMMIE NIGHT'. See following chapter for a description of bonfire night.

12. The lengthy court case that followed this incident revolved around who made the first move in this confrontation. It nicely indicates the importance of subjective interpretations of 'what happened'.

13. This statement of the 'entertainment' for the other residents illustrates one of the aspects of the neighbourhood event in Luke Street.

14. S. Cohen, op. cit. (1971) pp. 333–4.

15. The word 'start' was an important one in the boys' vocabulary. If either the boys or the police 'started' there would be 'trouble'. 'Starting' can be taken to mean initiating conflict.

16. C. Werthman, 'The Function of Social Definitions in the Development of Delinquent Careers in *Crime in the City* ed. D. Glaser (Harper and Row, 1970) p. 141.

17. Werthman also notes that 'Although the consequences of taking risks become more serious as arrest records get longer, a boy

who knows that the California Youth Authority awaits him if he is caught for theft or joyriding one more time can demonstrate possession of more courage than the boys who have never been caught'. C. Werthman, 'Delinquency and Moral Character' in *Delinquency, Crime and Social Process*, ed. D. R. Cressey and D. A. Ward (Harper and Row, 1969) pp. 613–32.

CHAPTER 8

1. 'Name for a species of drama popular in sixteenth century in which some moral and spiritual lesson was inculcated and in which the chief characters were personifications of abstract qualities'. Shorter Oxford English Dictionary on Historical Principles (definition first recorded 1765).
2. By no means all of those arrested came from the Luke Street neighbourhood however.
3. I was told, although I have no evidence to support this, that on the previous bonfire night the boys had sent a letter to the police requesting that for a whole week of bonfire night Luke Street should be regarded as a 'no go' area.
4. Much of the bonfire night action was mobile so Robbie's phraseology was apt.
5. Cohen talking about the mods and rockers battles of the mid-1960s says: 'The bulk of the young people present at the resorts came down not so much to make trouble as in the hope that there would be some trouble to watch. Their very presence, their readiness to be drawn into a situation of trouble and the sheer accretion of relatively trivial incidents were found inconvenient and offensive; but if there really had been great numbers deliberately intent on causing trouble, then much more trouble would have resulted.' S. Cohen, op. cit. (1972) p. 36.
6. My observation of these events indicated that it was the 'attitude' of the individual when confronted by the police after the event that was also of importance. Few of the boys when approached by the police were 'going to take it sitting down'.
7. This statement was common on the part of the boys in relation to incidents. At one level it can be taken to be a statement of fact; at another level it can be seen as an effective 'technique of neutralisation'.
8. This number of 400 is, I suggest, a gross exaggeration.
9. The theme of 'who's using who?' is an important one for analysing both relationships in the neighbourhood and

relationships with outsiders. If it is appropriate to talk of 'focal concerns' or cultural themes (cf. W. B. Miller, 'Lower Class Culture as a Generating milieu of Gang Delinquency', *Journal of Social Issues* vol. 15 (1958) pp. 5 – 19) then I suggest that 'who's using who?' was a focal concern in Luke Street.

CHAPTER 9

1. These observations are primarily based on the adult rather than the juvenile courts. I attended several juvenile court cases but this involved obtaining special permission and sitting with the court officials and social workers – a position I regarded as potentially disadvantageous to my contact with the boys.
2. This was referred to in Luke Street as 'witness talk'.
3. P. Cohen, op. cit. (1972) p. 133.
4. H. J. Parker, op. cit. (1974) p. 161.
5. A local solicitor was however in the habit of trying to arrange Luke Street cases to take place in a court outside Crossley in the belief that this 'stigma' of the area prejudiced the chances of his clients.

CHAPTER 10

1. This final statement nicely illustrates the way in which the children of the original Luke Street residents had maintained their housing class position and not sought accommodation in the area when it began to deteriorate.
2. Smith et al. note in their Manchester study 'They (the social workers) saw delinquency in the way that they saw maladjustment: as the result of a failure in social relationships, usually with the mother or the father, and although the solution to the problem did not always lie in family casework the dimension of family relationships could not be ignored. The importance of the peer group to the individual boy and the bad effect it may have had on his behaviour were functions of the failure of the family to be effective'. C. R. Smith *et al.*, *The Wincroft Youth Project: a Social Work Programme in a Slum Area* (Tavistock, 1972) p. 29.
3. See for instance R. Wilson, *Difficult Housing Estates* (Tavistock, 1963).
4. Peter Townsend, 'Area Deprivation Policies', *New Statesman* (6 Aug. 1976) p. 171.

APPENDIX

1. E. Liebow, op cit. (1967) p. 253
2. N. Polsky, *Hustlers, Beats and Others* (Pelican Books, 1971) p. 138.
3. N. Polsky ibid., p. 132.
4. There is also the recently reported actual British case of a female researcher who was involved in shoplifting. She told the judge at her trial that she wanted to experience what it was like to be a shoplifter and the judge said he would make the experience complete and gave her three months.
5. N. Polsky, ibid., p. 115.
6. L. Yablonsky, 'Experiences with the Criminal Community' in *Applied Sociology*, ed. A. Gouldner and S. M. Miller (Free Press, 1965) p. 72.
7. K. T. Erikson, 'A Comment on Disguised Observation in Sociology', *Social Problems*, vol. 14, no. 4 (Spring 1967) p. 368. See also L. Rainwater and D. J. Pittman, 'Ethical Problems in Studying a Politically Sensitive and Deviant Community', in G. J. McCall and J. L. Simmons, op. cit. (1969) pp. 276 – 88, and L. Humphreys, op. cit. (1970) pp. 167 – 73.